The Stability of the International Monetary System

The Stability of the International Monetary System

W. M. Scammell

Rowman & Littlefield
PUBLISHERS

ROWMAN & LITTLEFIELD

Published in the United States of America in 1987
by Rowman & Littlefield, Publishers
(a division of Littlefield, Adams & Company)
81 Adams Drive, Totowa, New Jersey 07512

Library of Congress Cataloging-in-Publication Data
Scammell, W. M.
    The stability of the international monetary
system.

    Includes index.
    1. International finance.   2. Foreign exchange.
I. Title.
HG3881.S334   1987   332.4'5   86-22004
ISBN 0-8476-7537-8 cloth
ISBN 0-8476-7541-6 paper

89 88 87
10 9 8 7 6 5 4 3 2 1
Printed in Hong Kong

Contents

List of Tables

Preface

This book reflects an attempt to answer questions put to me by academic colleagues (who were not economists) at a time when the international financial system was exhibiting symptoms of strain and disintegration. Is it possible that the international monetary system could collapse? Through what processes could disintegration take place? My answer was given in an afternoon seminar with non-economist social scientists and a few curious economist colleagues, quick to pounce on errors of fact or reasoning.

The discussion which took place convinced me of two things which led me to persevere and rescue some of that discussion for a wider audience. First, the nexus of relationships which we call the international monetary system can be, and indeed is, best presented in a set of verbal propositions intelligible to most thinking people and free from the mathematical encumbrances with which, nowadays, economists try to glamorise their matter. Second, there is, in any event, an obligation to expound the problem in this way if one wishes to reach the audience one should reach, namely politicians, bankers, journalists, teachers and academics with time enough to stop being specialists.

I have presented the argument in book form much as I did in seminar, untidily and with some, perhaps pardonable, exaggeration. If it continues to evoke discussion it will have served its purpose.

Hamilton, Ontario   W. M. S.
June 1986

1

Introduction

This book examines the international monetary system – a part of a wider and perhaps more acceptable conception, that of the international economy. Within the international economy, as a complex of trading relationships based on commodities, services, skills and factor exchanges and built up over centuries, there exists the complex of relationships by which such an economy is financed. As money forms a distinct concern within the exchange and production of any single national economy, the international monetary system has its own existence as an integral part of the wider international economy.

Within a domestic economic system we tend to regard the monetary system as a distinct entity, with its own institutions, its own problems of management and presenting policy-makers with its own propensities for instability and breakdown. Theory has not, indeed, unravelled the intricate skein of relations between the monetary and the real aspects of the economy. In the international setting, things are no better. The strands of cause and effect are longer and more intricate, the institutional framework more dispersed and the control problems more indeterminate.

The international monetary system is concerned with flows between nations of current and capital funds and with the relations between national currencies, central banks and monetary institutions. It is a misnomer to describe such a complex as a 'system'. To do so implies a mechanism of interlocking parts whose operation is known and predictable and in which changes can be made to achieve specified results. In our yearning for precision we stray into simplification. Nevertheless, the word 'system' is used, and we shall use it for want of a better.

In fact the international monetary system is a conglomerate, the

result of diverse foci of growth and development in which participants are for the most part unaware of any behaviour conditioned
by a system as such. •The international monetary system is an
aggregate of many national monetary systems whose relationships
have, at least until the present century, been conditioned mainly
by a few institutional contacts and practices operating under
conditions of trial and error. The nineteenth-century gold standard
was such a loose aggregation, in which the flows, the pressure
points, the reactions and probable results were tentatively discussed as the century progressed. Only since the Second World
War has the concept of an international monetary system crept
into the mental consciousness of bankers, economists, politicians
and international civil servants, quickening their thinking, planning and ideas. Probably they still imbue it with a greater integra-
tion, cohesion and malleability than is, in fact, its due. With the
risk that we prolong this error, we proceed.

The international monetary system is little more than a century
old. From the beginnings, in the middle of the last century, we
have recognised problems which formerly did not exist, or if they
existed did so only in such magnitude as not to command serious
attention – problems such as choice of an international monetary
unit, processes of foreign balance adjustment, adaption of financial institutions to evolving conditions and control of the system
from the centre. As the international monetary system has matured within the international economy these problems have become familiar, forming headings on the agenda of planners for
international monetary reform.

Throughout the century of its self-conscious existence the international monetary system has demonstrated both continuity and
turbulent change. There has been continuity in the sense that its
evolution can be historically traced and observed as having within
it features which are clearly fundamental and probably essential to
its existence, but which have expressed themselves in different
ways throughout its career. Despite two world wars, which shook
the international economy to its foundation, the monetary system
survived in its essentials, although both wars brought in their train
formidable problems of reconstruction and adaptation. There has,
therefore, been continuity in the sense that at no stage in its
development has the system incurred total breakdown. Even in
1944, when the Bretton Woods Conference had a unique and

never-to-be-repeated opportunity to reform and rebuild the system, the changes were structural rather than fundamental, the old categorical imperatives emerging as before. At the same time, turbulence has not been lacking. International monetary crises have been two-a-penny, from the Baring crisis of 1890 to the oil crisis of 1974. The 'currency question' no doubt caught the eye of Jolyon Forsyte turning the pages of *The Times* to check the price of Consols in 1880. The recycling problem was explained, somewhat obscurely, to television audiences in 1974. Crisis has not been the right word. If crisis be change, sometimes sharp and unexpected change coupled with risk and living dangerously, then crisis has not been the ruin of the international monetary system; rather it has been its dynamic.

Stability and instability have alternated in the international monetary system. From 1870 to 1914 the international gold standard gave to the system what was probably its greatest period of stability. The inter-war period, overshadowed by the breakdown of the gold standard and plagued by extreme economic nationalism, brought instability which imperilled the system. The Bretton Woods period from 1946 to 1971 was a period of tentative internationally organised planning which, coincident with economic growth, brought relative stability once more. The breakdown of the Bretton Woods system in the early 1970s ushered in a period of instability and improvisation which is still with us. In all of these periods, the problem of stability – namely the problem of preserving within the system an ability to adapt to both random shocks from without (what the economist would call 'exogenous forces') and developmental change from within (the economist's 'endogenous forces') – is fundamental.

In all the phases of development of the international monetary system there have been certain features within the system which are 'stability' conditions. In the present and in all future developments of the system these basic conditions must be met: failure to meet them means instability leading in the extreme to total breakdown. It is our purpose in this book to identify these stability conditions and relate them to the system as we now find it. This is an ambitious question. What we are really aiming at is to lay bare the principles for control of the international monetary system through policy, by whomever that policy may be administered.

Three subject-matters necessarily combine in a study of the

international monetary system: economics, for analyses of operations and institutions; history, for the record of the system in action; and politics, for the examination of motives and the processes of policy decision-making. In economics, examination of international monetary problems has been intense and continuous. Since the eighteenth century the problem of foreign balance adjustment has been examined. In the nineteenth century, consciousness of the gold standard as an international system provoked constant scrutiny and helped to evolve a general theory of price adjustment. Since the Second World War, Keynesian economics has extended itself into macro open-economy analysis. Balance-of-payments adjustment theory, exchange-rate analysis and capital-market studies have enormously enhanced our insight into the mechanisms at work in international finance. The blaze of interest in monetarism in the 1970s extended its glare to international economics and balance-of-payments analysis. A spate of books and articles covers the working of the system and the implications for reform of the system. In theoretical economics we approach the discussion of international monetary economics from a position of strength. There are, however, some weaknesses in our theorising which are hard to overcome. To begin with, the international monetary system is hard to model. Its very complexity and sprawling ramifications make it unsuitable for highly formal or econometric analysis. There are too many variables, too many stochastic terms, for a formal model to fulfil its dual purpose of prediction and control. The most useful theory we have on international finance comes not from theorising on the international monetary system itself but from examining the external aspects of open-economy macro models. Perhaps only in the field of exchange-market analysis have the mathematical economists found scope for their talents. For the international monetary system we can only say with Mr Bolfry that the world is too important to hand it over to men 'simply because they are good at sums'.[1]

In the field of economic history the affairs of the international monetary system have until recently not attracted much attention, but in the last decade there have been signs of awareness of the work which has to be done. Examination of international monetary crises of the past, case-study analyses, detailed documentation

---

[1]The devil, in James Bridie's play *Mr Bolfry*.

of monetary policies and of the issues of international conferences, are all beginning to attract the investigator. Availability of formerly secret documents is slowly illuminating events which were long the subject of speculative generalisations.[1] The facts establish themselves with a growing recognition of international economic history as a subject in its own right.

Within the subject of political science, study of international monetary affairs has had scant recognition. There have been notable survey studies[2] of a historical kind, but no serious effort to build up a political theory of the specific issues raised by policy-making, national or international. Let us list a few of the problems. First, there is the examination of the potential conflict of interest between pursuit by national governments of domestic equilibrium (that is, high employment with stable prices), and recognition and pursuit of international objectives, such as stable exchange rates, income-fluctuation transmission, and involvement in international co-operative enterprises, either of a regional or worldwide scope. The purely economic aspects of this conflict have long been bared for examination, but the conflict-of-interest problems are as much political as economic. Such problems we meet on an *ad hoc* basis, with no general principles for guidance.

Second, we should look for a close examination of international monetary co-operation. In this field we have felt our way forward for a century – through the accepted practices of the nineteenth-century gold standard; the treaty-making of the inter-war period

[1]For example, the American charge, that between 1932 and 1936 the British increased the competitiveness of their exports by covert depreciation of sterling with their new Exchange Equalisation Account, has been examined competently by Susan Howson, in her *Domestic Monetary Management in Britain 1919–38* (Cambridge University Press, 1975) almost as soon as Treasury documents became available under the 30-year rule. Light has also been shed on the politics of Britain's return to the gold standard in 1925 by other books written in the light of Treasury papers. The wartime negotiations for the Bretton Woods Conference, for lend-lease and stabilisation loans, the American genesis of the Marshall Plan – all these have received close attention.

[2]For example, Richard Gardner's *Sterling–Dollar Diplomacy in Current Perspective*, 2nd edn (Columbia Univ. Press, New York, 1980); Susan Strange's *International Economic Relations of the Western World, 1959–71, Vol. 2, International Monetary Relations* (Royal Institute of International Affairs, London, 1976).

and the grandiose essays in monetary co-operation at Bretton Woods; in the Group of Ten; and in numerous regional experiments such as the sterling area and later the European Monetary Agreement. It is inevitable that individual nations in their approach to international monetary planning should to some degree pursue their own economic aspirations. Unless an answer can be given to the question 'What is there in it for us?', co-operation can only be ephemeral. Now, in the cynical and aggressive mood of the Reagan/Thatcher epoch, the problems of monetary, indeed of any, co-operation seem tougher than they did in the early days of Bretton Woods and the Marshall Plan, but, if we are to survive, they must be met. The problems grow out of the heterogeneity of the economic and political interests of nations, but these no more imply the inevitable failure of monetary co-operation than the diversity of peoples, races and colours in the United States, Canada or the Soviet Union implies the failure of these nations as federal governmental systems.

Then, third, there is the question of national sovereignty in its relations to international monetary affairs. Hereto and at present, individual governments regard decisions on exchange rates, interest rates, and macro-economic policies for growth and employment, as sacrosanct – as inviolably national as decisions pertaining to peace and war. But for leading countries such decisions have immediate international repercussions and take their place in determining the condition and direction of the international economy. There is no escaping the fact that any true international payments system which is to endure for long must involve some loss of national sovereignty for participant nations. Any such system is likely to be a compromise between the extremes of a homogeneous world currency (which would of course mean complete surrender of national monetary control) and an uncoordinated congeries of separate monetary entities acting individually. The first of these is impracticable, the second intolerable. The problem lies in determining that degree of external authority to which member nations will submit and which will allow the system to function smoothly. To the solution of this problem the political scientist has as great a contribution to make as the economist.

Fourth, there is the difficulty, a political difficulty, that the nations comprising the international system are not homogeneous. We cannot see the Western economy (as, say, typified by members of the IMF) as equal partners in an international enterprise.[1] Rather, the component nations long ago developed the proclivity to congeal into groups of varying formality and cohesion. It is easy to observe at present the outline of such groups: the United States with Canada as its satellite, the European Community, the oil-rich developing countries, the poor Third World, and the Soviet Union and its supporters. For better or worse we must expect the international monetary system to have to operate within this framework. The parameters of this collectivity are political; the economic issues follow from them.

So in an examination of the international monetary system we have to combine our knowledge of the techniques of that system with the interplay of political motivations, all in the light of historical experience. This is difficult. It is a trick almost for gods, not men.

In this book we shall proceed in hopeful rather than godlike fashion, trying to ask the right questions and hoping for answers to be supplied from the three subject-matters we believe to be relevant. In the next chapter we will ask the question: what is fundamental in the international monetary system; what defines it, sets its limits and gives it continuity? Our test of such fundamental characteristics is that they are such that any failure to reproduce them, in any historical setting, will destroy or imperil the system. Once identified, these fundamentals dictate the format of subsequent chapters. After a brief historical interlude which places these fundamentals in the institutional framework of the system as it has evolved over the past century, and tries to understand their interplay and interdependence, we set about examining the funda-

---

[1] A major mistake in the Bretton Woods conception was made at the outset, when the suggestion of J. H. Williams to build the system around 'key currencies', thus recognising the importance of the dollar area, the sterling area, Western Europe and, one might have anticipated, the Third World, was ignored. Instead, the realities were side-stepped and a principle of equality was followed. Thus the Fund found itself the custodian of currencies which were useless as world liquidity and adjudicating upon exchange rates which in 70 per cent of cases were of no importance. The Fund has tried to break away from this by forming within itself negotiating groups such as the Group of Ten, but the adaptations have been of mixed usefulness: cf. J. H. Williams, *Postwar Monetary Plans*, 3rd edn (Knopf, New York, 1947).

mentals themselves. The ultimate purpose is to see how adaptable the total system may be while still conforming to fundamental necessities.

Along the way we have to pick up other threads to weave into the fabric. Economic ideas change. The central theory of balance-of-payments adjustment began with Hume, matured with Ricardo, and was given new starts and developments after Keynes revolutionised macro economics. In the 1960s and 1970s the new monetarism added its gloss to this important aspect of our subject. That contribution needs examination. This comes in Chapter 6.

Apart from the main argument, the reader may require guidance on some important institutional developments which in recent decades have given the theoretical problems that form the book's theme a change of setting. The changes which have taken place in the international capital market loom large in this respect. We evelute these changes in the text, the purpose being to sketch in necessary material which might be unfamiliar to the non-specialist.

The writer has had some doubts about the title of the book – the 'stability' or the 'instability' of the international monetary system. Clearly the choice might be one or the other for the same subject-matter. But the choice either way implies a conclusion. Is the vessel a poor sea-boat, surviving with difficulty in a choppy sea, capable of foundering at any time? Or is it a ship in good trim, capable not only of surviving but of adjusting to new sets of the wind and sea and keeping on course? The writer now inclines to the latter view; so we have settled for 'stability'. Perhaps by Chapter 9 he may have changed his mind. We shall see.

2

The Necessities of the System

(i) Introduction

An international monetary system must have four elements. First, there must be a form of international money usable by countries within the system for clearing residual balances with other countries, in which form reserves against this contingency may be held and with which a country's monetary authority may intervene to influence the value of its own currency in the foreign-exchange market. Second, there must be adequate institutional arrangements in the form of interrelated banking systems, money markets, foreign-exchange markets and the like, through which flows of international money may circulate within the system. Third, there must exist a method or methods through which the distribution of international money as between countries can be adjusted by acting upon their balances of payments. Finally, there must be some power at the centre of the system to influence the working of international monetary arrangements.

Each of these four elements has, of course, its own necessities which, in each case, enable it to function and play its part in the whole system. But one feature is common to all the elements and is ubiquitous in the whole. If the condition of confidence is not universally met, even the four elements are not in themselves sufficient to provide a workable system. There must be confidence of acceptability in the international money form whatever it may be; confidence in the stability of financial institutions of whatever form; confidence of the ability of countries to control their balances of payments to conform to a necessary behaviour pattern; confidence in whatever forms of international organisation may exist to control the system. Failure of confidence at any point in the system imperils the whole.

(ii) International money

To define the nature of money in a single economy is a simple matter. Money is that which the government of the country defines as such. The concept of fiat money is universally understood and accepted. Moreover, in most mature economies, what is defined as fiat money is confirmed by a long process of evolution and progressive acceptance. In the international monetary system there is no such simplicity. At whose fiat is international money to be declared so? Evolution of international monies has led in various directions. There are several candidates in the field.

History has given us three candidates: gold, convertible currencies, and the created liabilities of the IMF. Even to name these is to suggest at once deficiencies in their compliance with the definition of international money. Gold is limited in amount, and its value in relation to a constantly growing volume of world trade is inherently unstable. It no longer serves as an international unit of account, having been superseded by the US dollar and, latterly, by the SDR. It is long out of use as a means of commercial payment. It still holds a place, however, as a store of value and a vehicle of speculation. When we turn to convertible currencies, difficulties come thick and fast. First, we must ask: convertible into what? Not gold, for that throws us back to gold as the ultimate international money, which, *de facto*, it is not. Convertible, then, we say, into one another. If we can move freely and without risk of loss or gain from one currency to another, then we have achieved the ultimate and are ready for a single world currency, and in the meantime it is a matter of indifference which individual currency we use for transactions and hold for reserves. But currencies are only convertible into one another at risk. All are not equal; 'some are more equal than others'. If we argue that all convertible currencies are forms of international money, then we would do well to remember Gresham's law and its governance of the coexistence of more than one money form. Finally, turning to the created liabilities of the IMF, their money function is circumscribed. They form in the aggregate only a small proportion of what we term 'international liquidity', and although SDRs now serve as an international unit of account to the IMF, increase of their total amount *pari passu* with the expansion of world trade is impossible until they achieve that indispensable quality of any money form, universal acceptability.

There is a further difficulty. It has become conventional to describe international money as international liquidity. The two terms are not, however, interchangeable. International money may be precisely defined; its amount is ascertainable from a variety of statistical sources. It consists of aggregate central-bank exchange reserves plus immediate drawing rights on the IMF. International liquidity is a broader term, implying the total world means of sustaining balance-of-payments deficits without changes of exchange rates or the help of direct controls. It implies a broad spectrum of assets, shading from gold (with its vestigial use as a commodity money), through currencies, to less-tangible assets such as public and private sector credit, all of which may be mobilised by a country either to forestall a deficit in the net liquidity balance or to accommodate it by reserve movements if it occurs. The best formal way to handle this vagueness of nomenclature is to distinguish between first-line international liquidity, consisting of international money held in central-bank reserves, and second-line international liquidity, which not only supplements international money but may significantly diminish world demand for it. That the distinction between first- and second-line international liquidity is important and looms large in the pressure of the international liquidity problem at any time, is demonstrable by numerous historical examples. In 1913 and the years immediately prior to the First World War, the amount of first-line international liquidity (that is, gold in that historical context) was small,[1] but the world was not conscious of an international liquidity problem because, in a climate of political stability, trade credit was large and long, and long-term private credit was considerable. More recently, in the mid-1970s, the easing of the international

---

[1] In 1913, the level of gold reserves held by the Bank of England to underpin the world's leading currency was 5.3 per cent of the value of British imports. In the same year, total *world* reserve holdings (of gold and foreign exchange) were only 21 per cent of the value of world imports. In 1957, a year when the international liquidity famine was regarded as acute, the comparable figure was 51 per cent.

liquidity problem of the 1960s was due not so much to the more flexible pattern of exchange rates begun in 1970 as to the large volume of international private-sector lending which was a feature of this period.

The distinction between first- and second-line international liquidity is, therefore, no mere exercise in academic hair-splitting: the first is international money, the second is the cushion which eases the weight of demand for international money. Moreover it has significance for the problem of how we are to quantify international liquidity. We can only quantify what we can identify, categorise and measure. We have statistics for first-line liquidity easily available (cf. *International Financial Statistics*, IMF, Washington). We can have no idea what the volume of international trade credit may be at any time. We can only make wild guesses at commercial bank lending for stabilisation purposes, or the potential of governments for granting accomodation loans to deficit countries. We are totally ignorant of what countries may raise in foreign currencies through realisation of domestically held foreign assets. We can only say in retrospect (and often with surmise) that such forms of second-line international liquidity have been great or little in particular periods.

In the balance of payments as an accounting document the distinction between first- and second-line international liquidity is made at least with initial clarity. If we divide that document into its three sub-sections – current account, capital account and monetary movements account – the latter is concerned solely with flows of international money – that is, first-line liquidity. In the variations of exchange reserves and IMF positions in that sub-section the movements of the balance of payments are reflected. Here are the ebbs and flows of international money. In the capital account, and even in the current account, are reflected, though not directly in usable statistical form, such second-line international liquidity as may exist – the deferred credit for payment for exports and imports in the current account; the short-run money movements induced by interest-rate differentials in the short-term section of the capital account; the long-term private-sector loans in the long-term section of the capital account. Thus a balance of payments otherwise in deficit may have the deficit reduced or turned into surplus by inflows of short- or long-term capital deliberately induced by policies aimed at or capable of adjusting the deficit.

The relationship may be clarified as follows. If $(E\text{-}M)$ be the current account with E and M exports and imports respectively, and $(FB\text{-}FL)$ the capital account with FB and FL standing for foreign borrowing and foreign lending, then AF, the amount of accommodating finance required to clear the foreign-exchange market, may be added to give the balance-of-payments identity $(E\text{-}M) + (FB\text{-}FL) + AF = 0$. AF is first-line international liquidity. Second-line liquidity may be distributed between the other terms which determine the AF residual item. It follows also from this that the demand for international money for clearing international balances derives from (i) the total volume of international payments, and (ii) the degree of imbalance in international payments.

(iii) The institutional framework of international finance

The institutions of international finance have been in continuous evolution for several centuries, but not until the later nineteeth century, when world distances shrank with improved transport and communication, did the modern structure of the international economy emerge. Since then, development has been rapid and continuous. Banking systems have ramified, foreign-exchange markets have become more widespread and more sensitive, and national capital markets have blended and blurred with the establishment of a virtual international market in capital which has brought its own advantanges and problems. The institutional element of the international monetary system by its very speed of growth and increasing sophistication has had less than its share of attention, admiration being too often substituted for analysis. During the past decade, problems directly traceable to institutional weaknesses have made us less sure of the system's perfection.

The institutional assumption of economic theory pictures a world of homogeneous nation states each with its currency, banking system and central bank – the currencies being interchangeable in a worldwide foreign-exchange market. Reality forces upon us a somewhat modified picture. Some few key currencies with their banking systems and monetary policies dominate the scene. A few exchange rates are crucial, and the performance of key currencies as to their balances of payments does much to determine the stability of the whole system. With the influence of a key currency goes political power. Decision-making in the international monetary system is not within a multilateral system of many equal powers, but within a small coterie of governments whose influence and financial leverage dominates the system. Beside the key currencies are a score or so of vehicle currencies, in which routine intra-country payments are made but of which only working balances are held by the countries having need of them. Finally, there are many currencies, in excess of a hundred, which are either not traded on the foreign-exchange market or are traded only in a limited market for limited purposes, such as to enable foreigners to travel within the country. Typically such countries pay for their imports in the currencies of the countries from which they import, while looking for payment for their exports in a currency which they can use to discharge their own external debts. They may peg their exchange rate by defining their currency unit in terms of some other currency, and maintain that value by dint of exchange control. To them, their balance of payments is important as a key macro determinant of their economy, and they defend it to the best of their ability. To the international monetary system as a whole, neither they nor their currencies are of importance.[1]

The institutions of international finance, for the purposes of this brief discussion, may be divided into three groups: the aggregation of national banking systems, including the main central banks, commercial banking systems and the specialised international banking institutions which engage in overseas business; the foreign-exchange market dealing in currency titles for spot and

[1] It is surprising that as late as 1944 the Bretton Woods system was designed on the assumption of the equality in power, trade status, and financial influence of its members, rejecting the alternative key-currencies approach which was advocated by some economists at the time (cf. John H. Williams, *Postwar Monetary Plans*, 3rd edn (New York, 1944). The probable reason for the adoption of an 'equality' approach was that the Americans feared that a key currencies' approach would lead to Britain occupying, by reason of sterling as the leading key-currency, a place at the centre of the system. Whatever the reason, all countries and currencies were given equal status in the IMF (qualified only by the size of their trade), and that body received subscriptions ultimately in more than a hundred currencies which were useless as international liquidity, and presided over many exchange rates whose values were purely nominal.

forward trading; and the international capital market dealing in flows of funds for investment across frontiers. Within each of these groups we can only single out for attention such aspects as we may wish to refer to later.

The most important aspect of banking systems in their international setting is twofold. Central banks act as custodians, each for the international currency reserves of their countries, and operate in the foreign-exchange market on a scale greater than most private operators. Their decisions as to frequency and extent of participation in the market and their skill in conducting support operations are crucial for market stability. Second, there is the existence within large financial centres of a group of international banking institutions whose operations form a significant part of the international capital market. These centre themselves in London, New York and such cities as provide them with the specialised financial markets which they require for their operations. Their clients are mainly in the private sector and they concern themselves with directing flows of capital in accordance with the pursuit of profit and the minimising of risk. They are major participants in the foreign-exchange market. Their activities have internationalised the capital market during the years since the Second World War.

The growth and ramification of the international capital market in recent years is so important to the stability of the international monetary system that we shall return to it in a later chapter. At this stage we must note some of its effects. In the first place it has moved attention in balance-of-payments economics from the current account to the capital account. From the early days of balance-of-payments analysis the classical disequilibrium in that variable was seen as a short- or long-run disturbance to the current account, usually in the trade items, which was typically adjusted by changes in the capital account, or was met by measures to act upon the trade items, such as devaluation. As experience has accumulated we now see that disequilibrium springs often, perhaps more often, from the capital account. Capital movements are not always accommodating but are frequently autonomous. The greatly expanded international capital market has attracted funds in such volume that flows occasioned by profit potential or interest-rate differential demand such offsets elsewhere in the capital account, or if possible in the current account, as turn the older policy prescriptions on their head. Moreover, interest-rate policies, banking and monetary policies, determination of money quantity and other variables which were formerly seen in a domestic setting, now bulk large for the international system especially when they occur in one of the large countries.

A second feature resulting from the changes in the international capital market is the instability it may impart to the foreign-exchange market. The ease with which capital may be switched from country to country, the wide range of liquid and near-liquid assets available in financial centres, and the provision by technology of virtually instantaneous information, have all served to make capital more mobile. Shifts of funds in response to, or in anticipation of, events are now often so large as to make support of a threatened exchange rate by its parent central bank much more difficult than formerly. Conversely, speculative pressure against a currency may force the currency's external value above or below that which conforms with domestic policies, simply because the volume of speculation is beyond the power of the central bank to offset.

A third result of the great expansion of the international capital market are the doubts which now rise as to how national banking systems operate within it. In particular, doubts centre on the motivation and efficiency of the private-sector banking system, which now operates in a financial milieu more complex and dangerous than that of twenty years ago and which has been tempted into lending policies that may destabilise the whole system. Two factors have made this possible. First is the increased volume of available funds generated in the international banking system by the oil crisis of the 1970s. The liquidity of the banking system, particularly in the United States, led to lending policies which were unsound. Second, demand for funds by Third World countries did the rest. The international monetary system was left with a banking involvement of the rich countries in the unstable fortunes of the poor countries. In a period of rising world interest rates which made repayment and even servicing of such loans difficult and in some cases impossible, failure of banks through loan defaults became a major danger. It seems that there is always some new corner to turn. At a time when the American banking system appeared to be at last approaching maturity and matching itself to the responsibilities of underpinning an international currency, it succumbed to speculative and competitive profit mania in its loan policies, and demonstrated financial follies appropriate to a frontier society.

It would be unfair to limit our doubts as to the efficiency of the international banking system to the new and, in part, unfledged American system. The changes in the capital market and the harsher financial environment have produced strains in the British, West German and Italian banking systems. There have been failures and near-misses. It is clear that the increasing sophistication of the monetary system has in no way been accompanied by greater stability – rather the reverse.

(iv) An adjustment mechanism

Balance-of-payments analysis began with the concept of equilibrium in that balance. Any movement away from the equilibrium was said to set up forces which tended to restore equilibrium. Policy-making monetary authorities could supplement these built-in forces with their own policy measures. The so-called 'adjustment' of the balance of payments was thus in part automatic, in part a matter for conscious choice of measures by policy-makers.

All this was plausible enough. Under a gold standard a disequilibrium (typically a collapse of exports due to exogenous forces) would result in a loss or gain in gold, which created, either directly or through a fractional reserve system, a change in the domestic money supply. This, in conformity with the quantity theory of money, changed the relative price levels of domestic and foreign-traded goods which, in turn corrected the initial balance-of-payments deficit or surplus. Under a floating exchange-rate system a disequilibrium altered the exchange rate, changed relative prices and thus reacted upon the trade balance to correct it. In either case, adjustment through changes in relative prices acted through the trade balance and, subject to certain conditions,[1] corrected the

---

[1] The main condition was that of appropriate elasticity conditions of demand and supply prevailing for traded goods – the so-called Marshall–Lerner condition. Classical adjustment theory accumulated over the years a considerable body of literature, theoretical and applied, which cannot be reviewed here.

original disequilibrium in that balance. Keynesian income analysis, applied to balance-of-payments theory in the 1940s and 1950s supplemented the classical demonstration of the existence of powerful built-in stabilisers in balance-of-payments movements. In the 1960s, absorption theory and, later, monetarist ideologies added their contributions to the conventional wisdom of how to deal with the balance of payments. Since this theorising activated governments and central banks in their policies, it is worthwhile to summarise the main features of what might now be regarded as the conventional wisdom:

(1) Left to itself a balance of payments disequilibrium should eventually adjust itself.
(2) Since, however, the adjustment might be prolonged and painful and involve conditions which would not be politically acceptable, some interference with the adjustment process is justified.
(3) Since adjustment through changes in relative price levels, which works through a direct reduction of domestic prices themselves, is likely to create some unemployment, it is better to change relative prices through the exchange rate, i.e. by devaluation.
(4) The choices of a country facing a balance-of-payments disequilibrium (in the form of a deficit) are five in number:

  (i) if the country is well endowed with foreign exchange reserves and the balance-of-payments difficulties seem likely to be transitory, then the disequilibrium can be left to correct itself at some cost to the reserves;
  (ii) if the disequilibrium is in the current account, the country may seek adjustment by reducing its domestic price level relative to the price levels of its trading competitors; or
  (iii) the country may devalue its currency;
  (iv) if the disequilibrium is located in the capital account, adjustment may be sought by changing domestic interest rates relative to those abroad;
  (v) if none of the first four methods are acceptable, the country may resort to direct controls on current and/or capital account transactions. This choice, however, differs from the others in that it does not adjust the initial disequilibrium but merely suppresses it.

The relation between the adjustment process and international money is important. An international money serves to settle deficits and surpluses in the balance of payments when they arise. The adjustment system is designed to minimise these movements, to check and correct them and to invoke correctionary forces as disequilibrium occurs. When a balance of payments moves into deficit the ideal adjustment mechanism retards that movement, checks it and restores it to balance. In a perfect world it would not be necessary to provide international money at all, since perfect adjustment would hold all balances of payments perpetually in balance with no residuals to clear. In our imperfect world such precision and swiftness is not attained. The best we can say is: the better the adjustment system, the less the demand for international money. This is demonstrated by the fact that in past periods when the adjustment system was strong the international economy has been able to get along with a modest stock of international money. Conversely, in periods when the adjustment system has been weak, international money has been in short supply.[1]

Adjustment must be, and is, present in the international economy. If it were not, all international money would flow persistently to a few surplus countries and away from deficit countries, and thus ultimately the mechanism of payments would break down. Maldistribution of international money has often occured during the past century[2] but though it has induced strains in the international system it has not come to actual breakdown. The fact is that the internal stabilisers are strong but not so strong as to eliminate instability or to prevent disaster if they are persistently overriden by governmental policies.

[1] During the late nineteenth century when the international gold standard provided a serviceable adjustment system, the demand for international liquidity kept well within bounds. In the Bretton Woods period after the Second World War, the IMF so administered the adjustable-peg system as to remove the exchange rate as a tool of adjustment. At the same time, full-employment policies in the major countries precluded adjustment by price and income changes while demands for removal of trade barriers made direct controls on trade unpopular. Bereft of an adequate adjustment mechanism in a period of expanding trade, the demand for international liquidity became a major problem in the 1950s and 1960s.

[2] The flow of gold to the USA in the 1930s, the dollar problem of 1945–55, and the German surplus problem of the 1950s and 1960s, are obvious examples.

It is apparent from this discussion that the adjustment problem appears at two levels: at the level of the single country which must identify policies to control its balance of payments; and at the level of the world at large in which some 'system of adjustment' is necessary if individual national policies are not to be diverse and incompatible. So, for individual countries, adjustment appears in terms of balance-of-payments policies, often *ad hoc* and mercantilist in character, while for economists, interested in the wider problems of international stability, it appears rather as a mechanism through which certain accepted types of national balance-of-payments policies are harmonised, but which possess also the quality that, when disequilibria in balances of payments occur, forces within the system are invoked to correct them. Moreover, in looking at adjustment from both the national and global points of view we reveal a further problem in the policy field: since a country pursues policies for control of its domestic economy – policies aimed at employment, stable prices and economic growth – but also must pursue policies for balance-of-payments adjustment, how far are these policies compatible? Is there, in other words, a conflict between domestic and external policy aims? That such a conflict exists is well known and well documented in economic theory. The history of modern industrial states demonstrates the continuity of this problem. Three aspects of international adjustment therefore emerge: the national and international aspects and the problem of conflicting domestic and external policies.

In weighing the rival and often conflicting claims of domestic policies and policies to achieve balance-of-payments adjustment, an obvious starting-point is to ask the question: what forces impel a country to pursue balance-of-payments adjustment? In the case of a deficit, the deficit can only be sustained – unless the country changes its exchange rate or directly controls its imports – as long as its stock of international reserves holds out. In the case of a surplus, the forces impelling correction are not so strong. The surplus country may be content to accumulate reserves for as long as the surplus persists, resisting the demands of deficit countries for corrective action as long as these countries do not take retaliatory action against it. In a word, the sanctions operating against a surplus country to adjust its surplus are not as strong as those operating against a deficit country to correct its deficit. While it is argued that a balance-of-payments disequilibrium is two-sided and is the equal responsibility of surplus and deficit countries, it is usually upon the latter that the main burden of adjustment falls – if only because of the inadequacy of reserve holdings. It is, after all, always more pleasant to accumulate international money than to disburse it to other countries. The sanctions operating against a deficit country to adjust its deficit are real and pressing; those against a surplus country are largely moral and persuasive.

It should be obvious from this section that adjustment is a fundamental requirement of the international monetary system. Stability in that system is directly correlated with the presence and strength of adjustment forces and policies. But the harnessing of such forces and policies implies a multitude of choices. Both adjustment policies for individual countries and adjustment forces for the system as a whole imply choices for governments and choices for whatever group or entity directs the international system. The desiderata according to which such choices are made are diverse, confusing and unlikely to be interpreted with any degree of unanimity. This challenge brings us to the fourth fundamental requirement of the international monetary system: a directive force at the centre to identify the aims of policy and to co-ordinate the actions of the national and international participants.

(v) Control of the international monetary system

Leadership of the international monetary system is a political problem. Such leadership must deal with the functional matters already discussed: with the nature and supply of international money; with the forces and policies which determine the movements of balances of payments; and with the efforts of national policy-makers to achieve their several ends. Such leadership will give the system cohesion, welding it together and distinguishing it from a mere congeries of institutions and random behaviour patterns unworthy to be described as a system at all.

The history of the international economy over the past century demonstrates that such central control has been present in varying degree, and that the accepted success or failure of the system as such has been proportionate to its presence. During the gold-standard period (1870–1914) the system functioned effectively under the control of a few leading countries – a strange compromise between the gold standard of theory and the 'key-currency' arrangement later advocated[1] at the period of planning for Bretton Woods. 1918 to 1939 was a period of swift change, makeshift and improvisation in which control or co-operation in the international field was precluded by governmental clash in an atmosphere of fierce nationalism. The result in the monetary field was chaos and an approach to breakdown. The years after 1945 saw general recognition of the necessity for a central plan for the international monetary system. In the establishment of the Bretton Woods system, in the attempts by member nations to make it work, and in the establishment for the first time of many international monetary institutions, a will was demonstrated to seek international solutions to international problems. Certainly since the breakdown of the Bretton Woods system in 1971 there have been threats to the stability of the system, but they have been of a lesser urgency than those of the 1930s. The gold standard was a system of 'co-operating', Bretton Woods was (mildly) a system of control.

Between these extremes lies the solution to the problem of direction of the international monetary system. Between 'co-operation' and 'control' lies a long spectrum of compromises. It is best in examining these to start at the 'control' end. A completely controlled international monetary system must involve loss of national sovereignty. To be complete, central authority would have to encompass a choice of international money and control of its quantity, supervision of national decisions as to the values and variations of exchange rates – decisions affecting domestic levels of prices and income – and supervision of policies to be followed by countries for balance-of-payments adjustment. Given complete control of these matters there is no reason why we should not proceed to a world system with a single currency, centrally administered. The technical obstacles to such a state of affairs are considerable but surmountable; the political barriers are, however, insurmountable. The loss of national sovereignty involved in such central control would not be accepted by any government. Were it accepted by a government, that government would speedily be dislodged by forces and vested interests within the country. We are forced, therefore, by political reality to fall back upon a

[1]See footnotes – pp. 7, 14

centralised direction of the international system which falls some way short of the ideal – which partakes more of 'co-operation' than of central control. What characteristics must an acceptable and stable system possess?

First, it must involve some surrender of national sovereignty. National monetary authorities must be prepared to submit to some degree of external authority. Exchange rates, macro policies for control of prices and growth, interest-rate policies – these are the fields in which clashes in decision-making are inevitable. We shall not, at this stage, face the question of how such clashes are to be reconciled. Maybe they cannot. We can only say that the economic theory points the way we must go even if political reality blocks that way for the present.

Second, international control must involve sanctions which can be brought to bear against countries that abrogate agreed procedures or pursue unilateral policies. In the absence of such sanctions any international body or co-operative agency is foredoomed to failure at the first confrontation with a member or members. Such sanctions may vary in type and stringency. They may involve merely the publication of infringements or irregularities by a recalcitrant member, or they may be more extreme, consisting of the withdrawal of rights or privileges of membership. In the latter case the sanction becomes stronger the greater is the potential advantage to be had from participation in the general arrangement.

Finally, and to achieve the ultimate in international monetary control, it is necessary to recognise that such control is only a part of the wider problem of general international economic planning. It is not something which can be completely achieved in isolation. Money flows are in part the result of trade flows. If trade flows are perverted by controls and barriers then the payments flows are perverted. Only with a broad advance along the whole front of economic co-operation can monetary problems be prevented.

(vi) Economics and the political realities

The presentation of the international monetary system's main features in this bald and severe classification denudes the system of realism and overlooks features which have a bearing upon its stability. Although such features will find their way into later chapters it is as well to review them briefly to conclude this chapter.

The classification we have used portrays the system as an economic one and neglects powerful political forces which act upon the system and whose actions must be accommodated by it. Once we regard the international monetary system in a political as well as in an economic way, several considerations arise. The first is that in speaking of the 'international monetary system' we too often assume that system to consist of a multitude of nation states of at least some homogeneity. This it emphatically is not. The states are of different size and influence and are variously grouped either into sub-systems or into groups which act (or often act) as one state. Thus, we have at present: (a) that group of states which comprise the so-called free world – that is, states which are members of the UN and its agencies – which accept the principle of multi-lateral trade and have some regard to the price system and the advantages of free trade; (b) a group of collectivist and command economies which direct their foreign trade and control their foreign exchange and external pricing according to some master plan; and (c) a group of states, large in number and overwhelming in terms of population, in which per capita income is low and its growth retarded. In the face of cold war between East and West, confrontation between the economically developed and the developing nations, the existence of economic groups such as EEC, ECMA and the influence of agencies such as GATT and the IMF, the concept of free nations transacting on a basis of equality is far from reality. Yet much of the writing in international economics of the past quarter-century ignores these cleavages and groups, notes it merely in passing, and returns to the 'world' of exchange rates, balances of payments and international liquidity – to the comforting and familiar benchmarks which allow the construction of a consistent model. In relation to our central theme of stability of the international monetary system the political realities necessarily play a role, even a dominant role. The change of a tariff structure may change the direction of trade flows. The weakness of a currency may follow upon political decline, as has been the case with sterling. Nationalism expresses itself through many actions and policies in the monetary field.

Then there is the time element. The system as we have described it with its simple elements is a static one. What happens to all this when we think of the international system in its dynamic reality, with some countries growing, some stagnating, all changing at different rates? To fit the many variables of the international economy into a dynamic framework is impossible. Crude comparative status is our only alternative. One relation, however, between the international monetary system and economic growth should be noted: it is that an efficient international monetary system is essential to economic growth. If through an inefficient international monetary system growth in participant countries has to be checked by deflationary policies for monetary reasons, then growth is constrained and not diffused. The achievement of steady economic growth on a world scale depends upon an effective adjustment system for the balances of payments of countries which are growing – probably at different rates.

3

A Little History

(i) Introduction

History is the test-bench for economic theory. Denied the luxury of controlled experiment, the economist, liking to call himself a scientist, must resort to the record to seek confirmation of his analysis. In this chapter we will look at the main strands of change in the history of the international monetary system over the past century. We will not attempt a narrative of events, assuming that whoever is interested enough to delve deep into the working of that system is at least familiar with the main features of its development. Rather we shall divide the century since 1870[1] into three phases, distinguishable in retrospect by the adjustment arrangements for balances of payments governing the world system. These phases were:

(1) The international gold standard – 1870–1914 and 1925–31.
(2) Periods of flexible exchange rates – 1918–25 for virtually free rates, 1931–9 for flexible rates describable as a 'controlled float', and 1970 to the present for flexible rates uncertainly controlled by monetary authorities for more or less nationalistic ends.
(3) The Bretton Woods system from 1946 to 1971.

It would be true also in scanning these phases consecutively to see

[1]Why 1870? It is as good a date as any. In that year Germany completed her unification, the American civil war was over. The Western world entered upon a forty-year peace, with industrial and trade expansion and a 'system' of international payments which we have come to call the 'international gold standard'.

26

the world payments system in three conditions: (i) in the international gold standard as an unselfconscious standard which evolved of itself but which gave to the world system great stability; (ii) in the periods of exchange-rate flexibility as a system in flux, at one stage trying to find its way back to the earlier system of the gold standard, but at a later stage seeking to evolve into something new, dimly perceived but in greater accord with changing world conditions; and (iii) in an ordered system born at Bretton Woods in a never-to-be-repeated essay in international monetary planning. This classification of our development is hardly debatable. We adopt it because it is pertinent to our main theme – the stability or otherwise of the international monetary system. This is the variable that runs like a thread through all periods and phases.

(ii) The gold standard

What is the gold standard? An international payments system, a commodity base for a currency, a way to peg exchange rates, an adjustment system for balances of payments through changes in relative prices, a badge of financial conservatism and respectability. To the financial community of the 1920s it was the blessed pre-war normality to which they craved and engineered a return; to the sceptics of the 1930s it was the source of domestic instability, of depression and unemployment. To the critics of the Bretton Woods plans it was at once the feature which was missing from those plans and the feature which damned them by its inclusion. To the new Reagan administration of 1980 it was something to which America might return, a reflection of financial rectitude, the market system and the returning health of capitalism. It seems the gold-standard idea may be all things to all men.

For the purposes of this book we define the gold standard as a system of international payments in which:

(a) adjustment of national balances of payments has primacy over domestic policies aimed at price stabilisation or high employment of resources;

(b) changes in the trade balance are purposively met by induced changes in relative prices of traded and non-traded goods or changes in relative rates of economic growth;

(c) there is some machinery through which changes in trade balances invoke the appropriate domestic reactions in monetary policies; and
(d) exchange rates between currencies are held stable through universal definition of currency units in gold terms.

This definition of the gold standard is general enough to include a variety of sub-species which also fit the definition. If we take the gold standard of the nineteenth century (*circa* 1870–1914), then we have a system under which gold acted as an international money in terms of which all national monies were defined, thus holding exchange rates stable.[1] Deficits and surpluses in national balances of payments induced gold flows to the surplus and away from the deficit countries. Within the world system the distribution of money altered relative prices as the quantities of money altered, upward in the surplus, downward in the deficit countries. Changes in relative prices as domestic price levels changed, induced changes in the flows of traded goods which in turn adjusted the trade balance. Given the institutional framework and given a high price-elasticity of demand for imports and exports, the system would automatically move to keep balances of payments in equilibrium. Such was the theory.

Upon this basic theme there were (and are) many variants. Any international commodity money to which national currencies are tied would, with the observance of a few rules, produce this result. Equally, a system in which there is no international commodity money but in which national governments deflate their economies in response to a deficit and inflate them in response to a surplus, will have the same result. The repeated defence of fixed exchange rates during the Bretton Woods period demonstrated the widespread belief that price and income variations could still play a role in adjusting balances of payments. In the 1960s it came to be recognised that the Bretton Woods system as it had evolved was merely a gold-exchange standard in which the US dollar served as international currency for final settlement and national reserve holdings, and that currency in its turn was gold-based through the

---

[1]'Stable' but not 'fixed'. The gold points allowed a small variation of exchange rates both north and south of a fixed parity. This is a minor qualification.

US Treasury's obligation to purchase and sell gold at a fixed price. The Nixon Measures of 1971 not only ended the Bretton Woods system but ended equally the last institutional embodiment of the gold-standard idea.

Even without institutional framework the gold-standard idea died hard. It was conceded, even by the most militant of Keynesians believing in full employment and the divine right of nations to give precedence to domestic stability of prices and income, that self-induced price changes might play a useful secondary role in adjustment. Such was the doctrine underpinning the so-called 'stop–go' policies for balance-of-payments control by the UK in the 1950s and 1960s; such was the implicit belief of the IMF while advocating fixed exchange rates during the same period; and such has been the persistent advocacy by the IMF of domestic deflation as the panacea for deficits and external indebtedness by Third World countries in the 1970s and 1980s.

Picking our way between the pure gold-standard model and its variants we are struck by the way in which this model in some form or other survives. It is the institutional framework which has altered. The idea of adjusting the balance of payments by changing domestic prices and income relative to those of other countries remains. Clearly we must delve a little deeper if we are to understand why the so-called gold standard of the nineteenth century has been so lauded for stability while the latter-day applications of gold-standard theory have performed much less well and have acquired an unsavoury reputation.

The nineteenth-century gold standard was reputed to work as follows. A deficit country experienced an excess demand by its nationals for foreign currency to settle external debts. Finding the price of foreign currency rising, domestic debtors turned to their central bank from which, in conditions of full convertibility, gold was to be bought at a fixed price. A sustained deficit resulted, therefore, in an outflow of gold from the central bank, and since the gold holding of that bank was the base of the domestic money supply,[1] that supply would diminish. The domestic money supply was thus linked directly to the foreign balance. Given the validity of the quantity theory of money, so, too, was the domestic price level. Changes in the foreign balance would generate the changes

[1]Either directly or on a fractional reserve.

in domestic prices which would correct deficits and surpluses.

The most striking feature of this model is the primacy that is given to external stability. In the interest of balance-of-payments equilibrium at a fixed exchange rate, domestic deflations and expansions were to be tolerated and regarded as essential features of the system, despite any tendency they might have to accentuate cyclical fluctuation, intensify recession or create domestic instability. Although the period 1870 to 1914 was dominantly one of industrial expansion in the main trading countries, it was still punctuated by periods of recession. The 1870s saw acute industrial and agricultural depression; from 1870 to 1896 there was a secular decline of prices in the western world. Although the trend of world trade was upward throughout the period there were still fluctuations in balances of payments of individual countries. Yet there is little empirical evidence that fluctuations in balances of payments, or gold flows generated by them, set in train the recurrent sequences of events which gold-standard theory implies. Rather the reverse. Over the whole period between 1812 and 1912 the development of trade was gradual but increasing, and the general level of prices, while following the course of prosperity and depression, showed a marked docility of short-term fluctuation. The index number of wholesale prices rarely fluctuated by as much as 10 per cent in one year. Gold-standard adjustment if widely practised in terms of the theoretical model would surely have generated price changes more perceptible than this.

In fact, gold flows, when they occurred, were of much smaller amounts than the commodity trade balance might have led one to expect. Other and prompter forces accounted for the adjustment of balances of payments. A country with a commodity deficit loses money even before it loses gold. Domestic asset values fall as money leaves the deficit country, and thus interest rates rise. In the surplus countries, as money accumulates interest rates fall. As between deficit and surplus countries relative interest rates change, an international movement of capital is induced which compensates in the capital account of the balance of payments for the deficit in the trading account.

Institutionally and almost intuitively the system responded to the facts. The Bank of England was the centre of the later nineteenth-century gold standard and a fully convertible sterling its international liquidity. The Bank of England extended credit to other central banks. Its standing was considerable, its example studied keenly and followed in policy matters. By the fourth quarter of the century the Bank of England was using changes in short-term interest rates to draw short-term funds to London when these were necessary to adjust the balance of payments. Other central banks were quick to learn. The use of short-term interest rates to adjust balances of payments and to forestall major gold flows became general. Moreover, the Bank of England, firmly at the centre of the system, devised other methods for tightening its control over gold movements, allowing the form rather than the substance of a full gold standard to obtain.[1]

There can be no doubt that the international gold standard in its late nineteenth-century form provided the new industrial world with the most efficient system of adjustment for the balance of payments which it was ever to have, either by accident or by conscious design. It was this image which was to invoke emulation for the first quarter of the twentieth century, as the conventional wisdom evolved that to reinstate and prolong the gold standard was the theme of wise international monetary policy. What were the reasons for the success of this system?

Perhaps the first reason was the favourable financial environment in which it operated. The last major war in the west had ended in 1815. By 1870, labour and social unrest was quiescent. The hungry 1840s and Chartism, were matters of history. The American Civil War and the Crimean War were not of consequence for the world. In an atmosphere of confidence a second industrial revolution was accompanied by a burgeoning of world trade; while in the leading countries, Britain, France, Germany, the United States, stable political regimes were in control. In such an ambience a world financial community grew; grew as central banks grew, as banking systems expanded and connected and

---

[1]For detailed accounts of these developments, see Brian Tew, 'Sterling as an International Currency', *Economic Record*, June 1948; W. M. Scammell, 'The Working of the Gold Standard', *Yorkshire Bulletin of Economic and Social Research*, vol. 17, no. 1, May 1965; A. G. Ford, *The Gold Standard 1880–1914; Britain and Argentina* (Oxford, 1962). The standard works on the gold standard are: R. G. Hawtrey, *The Gold Standard in Theory and Practice*, 5th edn (Longmans, London, 1947); and W. A. Brown, *The International Gold Standard Reinterpreted, 1914–34*, 2 vols (National Bureau of Economic Research, New York, 1940). A useful recent addition to gold standard literature is Barry Eichengreen (ed.), *The Gold Standard in Theory and History* (Methuen, London, 1985).

capital markets became interdependent. It was the international financial community which made the gold standard possible. It is no exaggeration to say that the gold standard was an integral part of it. In at least two ways the system was favoured by its environment. First, the confidence which developed and became such a feature of this period enabled credit, and particularly international credit, to establish itself in many forms and, aided by the growth of capital markets, to provide a huge cushion of secondary international liquidity pre-empting the use of gold itself. In 1913 the world's gold stock was far below the level which, in later years, might have seemed appropriate to such a volume of trade. Confidence, the length and quantity of trade credit, made this possible. Second, the international financial community provided not only a framework through which the gold standard might function, but through which it could be controlled. Control, that elusive *sine qua non* of the international monetary system, was in this instance (a) achieved through obedience to a tacitly accepted set of rules of the gold-standard game, and (b) by being overseen by the Bank of England as central bank of the world's leading gold-based currency, held both as exchange reserves and as transactions balances.

Third, the gold standard provided in this period a satisfactory adjustment system for balances of payments. In the short period, current account deficits were met by changes in interest rates which induced equilibrating money flows in the capital account. Backing this short-term adjustment mechanism was the familiar gold-flow process of gold-standard theory acting more by its threat of use than by actual action. But there was still more to nineteenth-century adjustment. At the heart of the system was sterling's position as an international currency. Not only was sterling suited to its role by being fully convertible into gold, but it was by its nature free from recurrent scarcity or glut – the variations in demand and supply which might have rendered it subject to a confidence problem. By the very structure of the British balance of payments, scarcity of sterling was precluded by the fact that even in times of a favourable British trade balance sterling was still made available by the large volume of British lending abroad, both long- and short-term. Moreover, in the ebb and flow of the trade cycle the supply of sterling was rendered relatively constant by the inelastic nature of British demand for imports of food and raw materials. There was no tendency for wide British surpluses in recession to cause other countries to meet their deficits by direct controls on their imports from the centre country. The gold standard of the 1870–1914 period was a single-centred system based on sterling as a gold-convertible currency, administered by a central bank which for the time being was possessed of both the skill and the power to lead the system.

For a few decades all the conditions necessary for the smooth working of an international monetary system were satisfied. When, however, attempts were made to re-establish the gold standard after the Kaiser's war, not all the conditions could be met and the system failed. By 1925 when Britain returned to the gold standard and other countries followed, the international financial community with its attributes of confidence and political ambivalence had been replaced by rabid government-centred nationalism. There could be no acceptance of control of the system by convention, still less by a foreign central bank whose motives were no longer widely recognised.

So far as there was a plan for the new gold standard it was supposed that it would be around sterling that the new system would function. After all, Britain was the centre of the trading and sterling-using British Empire. Germany was oppressed by reparations payments and the burden of economic recovery from the war. France was unacceptable as a centre, and the United States, whose Federal Reserve system was in its infancy, was not yet ready. In Britain itself, a renewed gold standard, built around sterling at the pre-war gold parity, was regarded as desirable.

In April 1925 a qualified gold-bullion standard was set up[1] by the UK. Germany had led the way a year earlier. A number of countries followed, and by the end of 1925 thirty-five currencies, in addition to the US dollar, had either established gold parities or

---

[1]Prior to 1914, sterling was fully convertible into gold. Gold coins circulated within Britain on an equal parity with bank notes, and gold could be freely exported, imported and sold for coins at the Bank of England. The post-war bullion standard required the Bank of England to sell gold in 400-ounce bars at £3 17s. 10½d. per ounce. Coins were discontinued, but gold could be exported, and the Bank was obliged to buy all gold offered to it at £3 17s. 9d. per ounce. The backing for the note issue included a fiduciary issue which increased throughout the whole inter-war period.

stabilised their exchange rates for a long period. Within the period 1925–8 the re-establishment of the gold standard appeared to be virtually complete.

The new system failed. In 1931 Britain was forced to suspend gold payments and go to a floating exchange rate. She was followed off the standard by many countries. The so-called 'Gold Bloc' – France, Italy, Poland, Belgium, Holland, Luxembourg, Switzerland – lingered on precariously until 1936. With its collapse the gold standard as a conscious international experiment ended. What were the factors which brought about this failure?

First, was the unrealistic pattern of exchange rates at which currencies were stabilised and relative price levels supposedly expressed. The rates established were the result of separate and unco-ordinated acts by individual governments. In some cases, as with Britain, the parity chosen was that of 1914, despite four years of war, secular changes in trade and various rates of inflation. The result of these haphazard choices was that some currencies were overvalued,[1] some undervalued.[2] Each group of countries was thus left with domestic policies to adjust to the parity, such policies often being at odds with both the system and their own interests. Nurkse rightly said that it would have been better to set up the network of exchange rates 'by simultaneous and co-ordinated international action'.[3]

Second, financial confidence, which had been such a fixture of the old gold standard, was lacking in the new. The declared purpose of governments to return to gold at named parities had been barely achieved. The British, for example, had taken five years to achieve the desired $4.86 = £1, and had only done so as a result of speculative inflows of foreign funds into sterling as the desired level for pegging was approached. Almost every parity was established as a result of prolonged manipulation, and there was fear that many of the parities could not be maintained for long. As a result, political and economic events stirred up recurrent speculative movements.

Third, a large pool of 'hot' money now existed in the system to

[1]For example, Britain, Denmark, Norway, Italy.
[2]Germany, France, Belgium.
[3]Ragner Nurkse, *International Currency Experience* (League of Nations, 1944) p. 117.

make these speculative movements large and destabilising. Under the pre-war gold standard, international payments had typically been made by transfer of currency holdings in London. In the post-war setting, the London settlement monopoly was broken by New York and Paris, and dollar and franc deposits appeared in international clearing. There was now more than one financial centre. Each centre held sterling, dollar and franc balances in the others, and these were constantly being redistributed not only in accordance with trade transactions but in response to views on the currencies' prospects. Moreover, it was not only traders and commercial banks which held balances in other currencies. Central banks of many countries other than key-currency countries held their reserves wholly or partly in bank accounts and liquid securities in the key gold-standard countries. This was no more than the salient aspect of the gold-exchange standard which had been advocated in 1922 at the Genoa Conference as the form which the new gold standard should take. Nurkse lists thirty countries which held their central-bank reserves in the form of key foreign exchange. Once more, however, central banks were prone to reconstitute their reserves in response to changes in confidence, in interest rates, or in expectation of any change in the relation of a currency they held with gold. It was clear that in the event of any major threat to the gold-exchange standard, central banks would try to exchange that part of their reserves held in foreign currencies into gold. This did, in fact, happen in 1931 when events were thought to threaten the British currency and its convertibility into gold. The resultant gold loss through the summer of 1931 was instrumental in taking Britain off gold in September.

The fourth shortcoming of the inter-war gold standard was fundamental and likely to have proved fatal to it even if its other disabilities had not shortened its life. It failed as a mechanism for adjusting balances of payments. As such, one traditionally might have expected that (a) infows and outflows of gold should have been allowed to influence domestic money stock and thus to influence relative price levels, and (b) that outflows of gold should have triggered increases in short-term interest rates and inflows of gold decreases in such rates, both changes bringing about equilibrating capital flows. Essentially, whatever mechanism for adjustment was invoked it should have reflected the view that correction of foreign-balance disequilibrium took precedence over domestic equilibrium of prices and income. None of these conditions were met. Although empirical evidence is inconclusive it seems certain that in many cases governments were insisting upon their central banks giving primacy to domestic adjustment. There are many documented cases of central banks offsetting changes in their reserves, or of changing interest rates tardily or not all, in response to foreign-balance changes. The pattern that emerges seems to be one in which governments reacted to events by *ad hoc* policies rather than by gold-standard reactions. Moreover, such *ad hoc* policies, being unilateral and mercantilist in nature, were inimical to the gold standard as such.

To conclude, the gold standard of 1925–31 was a miserable failure, foredoomed by the conditions prevailing and by the lack of any central control over the system. With no adjustment system, disequilibria caused by diverse national policies inevitably became cumulative and brought the system to an end. It was in reality a period of pegged exchange rates (with some of the pegs at the wrong levels), and as such could not have been expected to continue for long. It showed extreme instability because all the stability conditions that we have distinguished were abrogated.

(iii) Flexible exchange rates

Before the Kaiser's war, the international monetary system had little experience of fluctuating exchange rates. The gold standard allowed only for movement of an exchange rate within a narrow band north and south of the gold parity, between the so-called gold points. These limits marked the point at which, for the nationals of a deficit country, depreciation of their exchange rate had gone so far that external debts could be settled more cheaply by exporting gold purchased from their central bank at the mint parity[1] – the cost of settlement including freight and insurance paid

---

[1]In the simplest case the gold points were determined by the cost, insurance and freight of gold exported or imported. In fact, central banks (including the Bank of England) had both a buying and a selling price for gold which widened the gold points still further. The Bank of England, seeing the advantage of limiting physical gold movements and sensing that the exchange rate could be set as an adjuster of the balance of payments, took to widening the gap between its buying and selling price for gold. Cf. Scammell, 'The Working of the Gold Standard', p. 40.

by the debtor. Apart from movement within this narrow band, exchange rates were regarded as immutable. It was to preserve their stability that gold flowed and adjustment (other than exchange adjustment) took place. During the war years the gold standard was in abeyance. In Britain, the forms of the gold standard – that is, the right of the public to buy and sell gold at the Bank of England and the right to export or import gold as settlement of external debts – remained, but were not practised for practical and patriotic reasons. On the continent, the gold standard also evaporated in the face of physical rather than legal impediments. In the United States, the legal forms were maintained at least until American entry into the war in 1917. Thus the outward appearances of the old system, in particular fixed exchange rates, remained in place, giving a false sense of normality, or at least of a state to which things could return. Fixed exchange rates were initially maintained by induced and 'voluntary' surrender of gold and foreign securities to governments by patriotic nationals. Only in January 1917 did Britain begin to appropriate gold and foreign assets from domestic holders. France did not use compulsion; Germany resorted to it in March 1917. By various means the leading countries supported throughout the war exchange rates appropriate to the summer of 1914. By the end of hostilities the international monetary system had a pattern of fixed exchange rates reflecting not the relative price levels of 1918 but of the pre-war world. The hope soon became prevalent that this familiar pattern of exchange rates would become the basis of a rehabilitated gold standard.

The period of floating exchange rates which followed the war was notable for two features. The first was that for the major countries the central thrust of international economic policy was to return to the gold standard at parities of currencies with gold that reflected the old exchange rates, even if this meant a long and painful process of deflation of domestic prices and costs. The British case was typical. The wartime peg on the pound–dollar rate was removed on 20 March 1919, and by mid-1919 the rate had fallen from \$4.86 = £1 to \$3.40 = £1. The British task in following the Cunliffe Committee's recommendation to return to gold at the pre-war parity was thus to deflate British prices relative to those of the USA in order to regain the pre-war purchasing-power parity. This process of deflation was in accordance with gold-standard precepts: the aim of external stability – in this case the exchange rate – was overriding, and domestic stability, even to the extent of breaking the post-war boom by purposive deflation of prices, income and employment, was to be sacrificed to it. There was no manipulation of the exchange rate by central-bank intervention in the exchange market.[1] Rather, the exchange rate was to be the passive barometer for changes in relative prices and the measure of progress towards the desired purchasing-power parity.

The second aspect of the free-exchange-rate condition of this period was the lack of any precedents for what was taking place. There had never before been floating exchanges. The uncertainties of the condition were many, and there was, in the beginning, no forward market in which to hedge against those uncertainties.[2] The idea of leaving the balance of payments to be adjusted by exchange-rate movements was never taken seriously. Floating exchange rates were regarded as an unfortunate interlude before return to a stable gold standard on the pre-war pattern – whatever that might have been.

Apart from freedom of exchange rates, the period from 1918 to 1925 was one of great instability in the international monetary system. This was due to the aftermath of the war: to outstanding war debts, reparations, changes in national financial strengths and, above all, mistaken national monetary policies.[3] But in terms of the requirements of an international monetary system (set down in our previous chapter) the confusion was also due to the fact that the four conditions necessary for an efficient international monetary system were now not met. Take them one by one. The most striking lack was that of a controlling force at the centre. More than any other condition floating exchange rates requires such a control. In its absence unilateral policies for influencing exchange

[1] The only sign of Bank of England intervention was a slight variation in the timing of purchases of US and Canadian dollars to service American debts. The Bank of England gold reserve hardly changed between 1920 and 1925.

[2] It is interesting to read Keynes's chapter on the evolution of a forward market in what is, to the author, one of Keynes' most striking and original books, *The Tract on Monetary Reform* (London, 1923) – see especially chapter 3.

[3] In particular, the British decision, taken at the behest of the Cunliffe Committee (cf. Committee on Currency and Foreign Exchanges after the War, First Interim Report, Cd. 9182, London, 1918) to return to the gold standard at the pre-war parity of sterling with gold and the dollar.

rates are likely to appear. Competitive depreciation and 'managed' floating quickly follow. In the 1918–25 period, however, exchange rates were not manipulated. Rather, they were the reflection and indeed the aim of manipulation of relative price-levels. Moreover, exchange-rate manipulation was precluded by the absence of any understanding or banking machinery for official intervention in the foreign-exchange market. The competitive depreciation was not of external money values but of domestic money values. For five years, from 1920 until April 1925, the British and American price levels were manipulated by their several governments until their relative alignment came near to the desired \$4.86 = £1 at which return to gold parity was planned. Throughout this period there was no co-ordination by governments of efforts made by individual nations to return to gold. Declarations of intent were made at the Brussels and Genoa Conferences but there was no central direction of the transition. The international financial community had been disintegrated by the war. It soon became apparent that the international financial system was not going to slide easily to a self-directing gold standard under British hegemony. The rules were different; even the figures on the international scene were different. Before, it had been central bankers and financial *cognoscenti* who, ruled; now it was governments, represented by officials and politicians who were short on technical expertise but long on chauvinistic self-interest.

Then there was the question of what was to act as international money. Contrary to what was believed in London, it could not be gold-backed sterling. The war had destroyed British financial supremacy. Secular changes in British trade and industry had been accelerated. The structure of the balance of payments had deteriorated by changes in the trade account, the invisibles and the capital account. There were even signs that the British experiment in free trade had begun to dissipate itself. But more than this the growth of the American dollar threatened sterling. Since 1914 the USA had become a creditor nation; its banking system, for long chaotic and unreliable, was being strengthened after 1913 by the new Federal Reserve System. The favourable trade balance of the war years and US lending overseas had honed new financial methods and institutions. The United States had become a new international financial force. But it was one of the ironies of this development that although ousting Britain from financial leadership the USA was not yet ready to assume a leading role. In the period 1918–25 and indeed in the late period of floating exchange rates from 1931 to 1939, there was a gaping hole at the centre of the international monetary system. The old leadership was gone; the new was not ready. The old international currency, even when gold-backed, was incapable of providing the new gold exchange standard with a centre reserve currency.

Finally, it is an understatement to say that under floating exchange rates between 1918 and 1925 an adjustment system was lacking. Had there been such a system it should have operated through market movements in the exchange rates themselves. The normal picture of an exchange-rate adjustment system is one in which deficits on trade account are adjusted through changes in relative price-levels reflected in exchange-rate changes. Here, as we have argued, the policy was rather to change relative price-levels themselves until these created the trade balance which would establish specific exchange-rate relationships. Adjustment was set aside in the interests of this policy which, as events later demonstrated, was doomed to failure.

Thus during the 1918–25 period of exchange-rate freedom the three principal requirements of a stable international monetary system were lacking. Moreover, the confidence of the pre-1914 gold standard was replaced by a groping uncertainty which compounded the difficulties of the system. We cannot regard the 1918–25 conditions as constituting an international monetary system in the sense in which we have defined it. Rather it was a transition to what the financial planners of the day regarded as a rehabilitation of the pre-war gold-standard system.

The fluctuating exchanges of the 1930s differed from those of the 1920s in several respects, but in none more than that the former were regarded as the new norm. Those of the 1920s had been seen as a tiresome transition condition soon to be set aside when the gold standard was restored. They were not a condition worthy of study in themselves or as candidate for a new monetary system. After 1931 it was clear that the gold standard had failed. The alternative was floating rates of exchange. It was a new game to be learned. What were the rules? How would the players behave?

In one sense this difference of attitude was the best attribute of the new monetary epoch. It meant an end to passivity, to a desire to have a manipulated monetary system rather than one which was supposed to be automatic and to whose working all members were to be subservient. Although there was to be a period of chaos and conflict of national policies, it was to be realised that unity of purpose and international monetary planning were possible. In two stages – in the Tri-Partite Monetary Agreement of 1936, and in the Bretton Woods Agreement of 1944 – progress was made, first to the definition of aims through treaty and second to a full-scale exercise in international monetary planning.

First, however, the world was to have its taste of monetary chaos. Between 1931 and 1936 all the requirements of a stable international monetary system were absent. Moreover, the world was in the grip of the greatest depression of modern times. For rational external policies were substituted actions which were diverse, conflicting, opportunistic and expressive only of *sauve qui peut*. Between April 1929 and April 1933 over thirty countries left the gold standard. Some countries freed their exchange rates, others stabilised in terms of a key currency such as sterling. The first effect of the gold-standard failure was to divide the world into currency blocs: the sterling bloc;[1] the gold bloc, a rump of nations still holding to a gold parity (until 1936); some Central European countries, notably Germany, who were to resort increasingly to direct controls on trade and payments; and the USA, still holding to a dollar parity with gold, and with limited gold-standard appearances in its currency management. The rivalries of these groups, especially between Britain and the USA, were a depressing feature of the period. All had different general considerations overriding their national policies. The British were anxious to strengthen an economy in the grip of long-term secular decline and to maintain sterling as a key currency; the satellite countries of the sterling bloc were concerned to stabilise their external payments in one earnable currency within as large a multilateral clearing area as possible; the gold-bloc countries struggled with an increasing overvaluation of their pegged currencies; the Central European countries dealt with surging German recovery and rearmament; and the USA sought by economic isolation and the domestic New Deal to lift itself out of the deepest depression in its history.

[1]Consisting of the British Commonwealth and empire, less Canada, plus a changing group of countries much of whose trade was financed in sterling.

Clashes inevitably occurred. The most significant was between Britain and the United States. Freed from gold in September 1931, sterling fell 10 per cent in relation to the US dollar. Five months later, in February 1932, the British established the Exchange Equalisation Account (a department of the Bank of England) to intervene in the exchange market, ostensibly to smooth the short-term movements of the sterling rate, but in the American view to help depreciate sterling in order to rebuild the sagging British export trade and pull Britain out of the depression.[1] The USA retaliated by setting up the American Stabilisation Fund in 1934, stocking it with dollars which were the accounting profit of the American devaluation of the dollar in that year. Between 1934 and 1936 there was a virtual stand-off between the two countries in the now unequal contest of rival exchange-rate management. By 1936 the principle of government intervention in what was supposed to be a free exchange market was well established. But 1936 also saw recognition that application of the principle could be overdone. In that year the gold bloc collapsed, and several of the participant countries, now on floating exchange rates, established their own exchange funds to 'order' their exchange rates. The British and the Americans had already had four years of 'management' of exchange rates, either for their own purposes or to forestall the purposes of the other. They now took the view that a world of six exchange funds each pursuing its own aims was unacceptable and might bring a final descent to anarchy. The Tripartite Monetary Agreement of 1936, which defined desirable co-operation between the British, French and American exchange funds, may be interpreted as an intuitive recognition that unilateral policies acting through free exchange rates had been carried too far. Some co-ordination, not to say control, of such policies was in order.

The experience of free exchange rates between 1931 and 1939 has often been invoked in later discussions of the efficacy or otherwise of free exchange rates as an adjustment mechanism of balances of payments. The fact is that lessons drawn from the history of this period are misleading. First, exchange rates were

[1]The merits and demerits of this view have been much debated. Certainly Britain pulled out of the depression more quickly than the USA, and that the British Treasury was anxious for the sterling rate not to rise is borne out by empirical work done by Susan Howson, in her *Domestic Monetary Management in Britain, 1919–38* (Cambridge, 1975) ch. 5.

free only in the sense that the fixed parities of the short-lived gold-standard experiment had been abandoned. The rates which followed were influenced by national exchange funds and were in fact 'controlled floats' in the later jargon of the subject. Second, the exchange funds themselves were unskilled and had no fixed procedures to govern them at least until the 1936 Tripartite Pact. If we accept the arguments of supporters of a free exchange market that such a market requires that all major participant countries allow commercial forces in the market to work themselves out freely, then it follows that any attempts by major countries to influence the market supply spread, either through retaliation or need for defence, until the whole market is no longer free but is controlled by a diversity of forces. In such conditions breakdown is inevitable and is only avoidable by a resort to co-operation. That is what happened in 1936, and the lesson was well enough learned for co-operation to be reinstated in 1942 during the planning of the Bretton Woods Agreement.

A third period of fluctuating exchange rates deserves attention: from 1970 to the present. When the Bretton Woods system ended with Nixon's decision to devalue the dollar, some countries had already abandoned the adjustable-peg system, and others were quick to follow.[1] Within a few years a familiar pattern emerged: leading countries allowed their rates to float but subjected them to considerable control by official intervention in the currency market. A number of other countries pegged their currencies to a key currency of their choice;[2] some pegged to the mean value of imaginary baskets of major currencies. A large number of countries administered their currencies, conducting their external trade in a major currency of their choice while providing their own currencies only for tourism and travel within the country, usually at a high exchange rate. By 1975, the eleven 'vehicle' currencies within the IMF that were floating accounted for almost 70 per cent

---

[1]The Canadians led the way by floating their dollar on 1 June 1970; Britain floated sterling in June 1972. The Japanese yen and Italian lira floated after the Volcker Agreement in February 1973. Among the last to quit a fixed parity were the USA and the 'Snake' countries in Europe in March 1973.

[2]A vestigial sterling bloc pegged to sterling, a number of countries followed the US dollar, some North African countries pegged to the French franc.

of the trade of all members of the Fund. The 'dollar standard' was over and had been replaced by a system of managed floats.

As with the previous various stages of international monetary history we will not attempt a narrative of events for the years from 1971 to the present. To readers of this book the benchmarks of this period are familiar: the attempts to stabilise the US dollar; the first oil crisis of 1973–4; the recession of 1974; the second oil crisis of 1979, and the deep international recession which followed it; the improvisations in international monetary matters to accomodate these events. It is more serviceable to summarise the changes and major features which manifested themselves in this period. We may wish to make use of these features in subsequent chapters.

(1) The fluctuating exchange rates to which the world reverted after 1970 were not the same as those of 1918–25, which were regarded as barometers of national price-levels and not as adjustment media to regulate balances of payments, nor those of 1931 to 1939, which were regarded, in the main, as variables to be regulated in the interests of domestic policies for industrial survival, growth or mercantilist ends in general. The post-1970 rates were typically regulated by national exchange funds in order to hold the rates steady for periods at levels which appeared for the moment appropriate to balance of payments. From time to time a rate would be allowed to move fairly freely until the exchange fund could stabilise it at some new and seemingly appropriate level. The net effect was thus to achieve a pattern of rates which was fairly stable in the short term (months) but might change a good deal from year to year. It is an interesting reflection that this exchange-rate pattern was not unlike what Keynes and White wanted for the IMF but which under the encouragement of that body congealed into a system of fixed rates.

(2) The fluctuating exchange rates of the 1970s proved to be more volatile than had been expected. In moving from level to level there was a distressing propensity for rates to overshoot what might have been presumed to be their purchasing-power parity level. This could be explained partly by the fact that equilibrium purchasing-power parity rates are conceivable only in situations where traded goods and services and their prices sets the rates whereas it was now capital movements which moved rate levels, and partly by the fact that once the international capital market awoke to the new dynamic it became evident that speculation

might be profitable as rates sought their levels. In fact, the exchange-rate movements of the 1970s resembled the automatic gear-box of a climbing car in which the gear shifts continually, seeking the most comfortable ratio only to be shifted by a new change in the gradient.

(3) It is conventional in balance-of-payments theory to talk of disequilibrium springing from changes in the current account, and to consider adjustment in terms of changes in the capital account. In the most recent period, disequilibria frequently had the capital account as the prime mover, and adjustment was often hard to find since it would have required movements in the current account which were either too large to achieve or would have required a change in the fundamental structure of the country's trade. This reversal of conventional theory has been caused by the enormous growth of the world capital market and the volume of funds which move in it. Often the proportion of currency trading in the total world foreign-exchange market that is accounted for by real trade transactions, is small.

(4) From (3) it follows that the volume of capital transactions which may be generated by speculative motives is also very large. It has, in fact, been frequently and increasingly demonstrated that the amount of 'hot money' speculation against a currency is often too large for a single central bank, however powerful and well endowed with reserves, to offset by its own operations in the market. The lesson is that when a currency is under speculative attack it cannot be defended by the old simple intervention methods.

(5) It has always been an economic truism that complete control of world exchange rates requires a co-ordination of national macro-policies across the main countries involved. To put the matter at its simplest, if all countries inflate or deflate together, exchange rates are stable, if they inflate and deflate diversely, exchange rates vary in response to the magnitudes of the divergences of income movement.[1] There should ideally be concerted policies for growth between the major countries. Instead, macro-policies are decided nationally and *ad hoc*, events as often

---

[1]France, under the Mitterand government, learned this when it tried to inflate its economy relative to a deflating USA, Britain and other countries. The result was a devaluation of the franc and a *volte face* of French expansionary policies – a bad blow for a socialist government.

as not throwing up some maverick such as the United States proved to be under Reagan in 1984 when a simple Keynesian boom (generated by defence expenditures) pulled the USA out of recession. This occurred simultaneously with continued recession or slow recovery in other countries and caused the dollar to become for the time being the world's strongest currency.

(6) Throughout the 1970s and 1980s there has persisted what may be described as a 'gold-standard mentality' among the policy-makers of main countries. This has manifested itself in the determination to seek economic stability by deliberate policies of financial restraint and deflation. The economic values of the early 1930s, which met depression by curtailed expenditures and high levels of saving, were revived. Monetarism and so-called supply-side economics were invoked to give academic respectability to policies which uniformly served to prolong depression and, in the British case, well-nigh destroyed the industrial structure. The Reagan administration, in its early restrictive phase, even flirted with the practicability of restoring the gold standard, for no better reason, it seems, than that the system had about it an aura of monetary rectitude which had an appeal to simple Republican minds. The IMF has been consistent in wishing upon every country which has been an applicant for its assistance, a uniform policy of deflationary adjustment – instant currency devaluation, a balanced budget and a package of deflationary reductions in government outlays and consumption. The past decade has demonstrated that in a world which for long imagined it had the key to full employment and growth there is still a capacity for economic self-destruction, which combines with economic ignorance to produce disastrous results.

(iv) The Bretton Woods system

So much has been written about the Bretton Woods system that we may here be brief. One thing can be certain: its dates. It began with the setting up of the IMF, which began business in March 1947, and it ended with the Nixon measures of August 1971. Thus it endured for a quarter of century, only a decade short of the nineteenth-century gold standard if we date that system from 1870 to 1914. True its longevity was not due entirely to its own merits.

For approximately its first ten years it was supported, indeed almost replaced, by institutional machinery designed to deal with the dollar shortage and the difficulties of transition from war to peace. It is arguable that the Bretton Woods system as Keynes and White designed it only began in earnest in January 1959, when general convertibility of currencies was achieved.

It is arguable, and the present writer would argue, that the Bretton Woods system was a successful experiment in international monetary planning. No system can be expected to endure for longer than it did in a world of bustling change and political transition. That it lasted throughout the post-war period of recovery and growth and was only superseded when the international economy exhibited fairly fundamental change, and that some aspects of it are vestigial in the present set-up, is indicative of its qualities. We shall look at the Bretton Woods system briefly in the light of the four necessary fundamentals we have derived. Its stability will be found to come from its recognition of these fundamentals; its instability to derive from its failure to fulfil them completely.

First, we look at international liquidity. The Bretton Woods system was set up around the IMF whose major function was to augment the national reserves of gold and exchange currencies of its members. Since gold was still a commodity money, and since the US dollar was the leading world currency, and was convertible into gold at a fixed price, it was inevitable that the system, in its international liquidity aspects, should resemble a gold exchange standard.[1] A key currency and gold were interchangeable as international money, and stocks of both were held by the Fund as well as by its members. It was as a gold exchange standard that Bretton Woods functioned in the 1960s, and it was as such that it failed. But in a broader sense the Fund never got it right so far as international liquidity was concerned. It was cursed by having a supply of all members' currencies, most of which were quite

[1]The resemblance of the Bretton Woods system to a gold standard was not seen by its founders, although it was observed by some of its critics at the planning stage. The system's gold-standard attributes were most marked in the 1960s when the USA dominated the system and its difficulties in preserving its convertibility at a fixed gold parity were evident. Indeed, failure to maintain the gold parity of the dollar at $35 per ounce was a prime cause of the ultimate breakup of the system.

useless to it; and it was short of dollars, the one currency required for the success of the system. Even with repeated increases in members' quotas, with the General Arrangements to Borrow of 1960 and with the Rio Agreement of 1967 to set up the SDR system, it was only the turnover to flexible exchange rates in 1970 and the flush of petro-dollars in the mid-1970s which set the problem to rest – for the time being.

Second, there was the failure of Bretton Woods to supply any adjustment mechanism. The original conception of this by Keynes, White and the founding fathers, was that, in the short term, exchange rates within the system should be fixed, and that balance-of-payments disequilibria should be met by reserve transfers, supplementable by drawings on the Fund. In the long run, exchange rates were to be variable to meet structural disequilibria. This model might have worked well enough had not the Fund built itself into a fervent espousal of fixed exchange rates – particularly opposing frequent changes of key-currency rates. This left the system without an adjustment variable. Exchange rates were to be fixed. Domestic levels of prices and costs were immune from manipulation in a Keynesian world hell-bent on full employment. Direct controls on the balance of payments were precluded by GATT and by Fund provisions. In these constrained circumstances the demand for international liquidity to finance disequilibria was maximised, and it was no wonder that this was the central problem of the system. It was only the fact that the period 1955 to 1965 was a period of sustained, crisis-free growth that enabled the system to work as well as it did. As soon as the pressures of the later 1960s – growing inflation, key-currency weakness and the American deficit – intensified, breakdown became inevitable.

Third, the control at the centre was inadequate. Sensing the indispensability of this the IMF had been placed by the planners squarely at the centre of the system, to be buttressed by other international organisations such as the World Bank and the International Trade Organisation. But things turned out differently. The World Bank was slow to start and its aims in the international capital field were limited. The ITO died at birth and was replaced by GATT. A plan for international co-ordination of national macro-policies came to nothing. As for the Fund itself, its authority was limited. During the period of Marshall Aid (1948 to 1952) it was thrust into the background, and organisations like

OEEC and the European Payments Union took the centre of the stage. Thwarted of its central role the Fund languished, fought minor battles with members on such matters as multiple gold prices, opposed any attempt on the part of members to free exchange rates, and demonstrated a strong American influence on its affairs. It returned to the centre in 1959, a rather different organisation than had been anticipated.[1]

Nevertheless, the Fund was intended to be the centre of the international monetary system, and would have been described as such by most observers in the late 1950s, through the 1960s, and for a part of the 1970s. What went wrong? Perhaps more than anything else it was that the idea of Bretton Woods as a new world system died with the founders. Keynes and White, its planners, had no say in its operation. They were succeeded by men of more limited horizons, who saw in the Fund a single financial institution responding in an *ad hoc* way to changing circumstances. American influence in the Fund, always strong, increased, and could, in the most charitable view, be described at best as well-meaning. Finally, the Fund's removal from the centre during the Marshall Aid period (1948–52) deprived it of power. It ceased to supply international liquidity to countries in receipt of Marshall Aid, and since it had nothing to give it had no sanctions against countries which refused to conform to the system. It was not until the later 1950s that strong leadership and liberal disbursals of funds placed it in a commanding position. It tried to assume the role of leader in the system, but it was too late. In none of the great monetary problems of its period (1947–71) did it lead or demonstrate the ability to lead. It made its contributions, but they were peripheral rather than central.

In the last decade of Bretton Woods (1959–71), the system became in all its essentials – save one – a gold exchange standard. At the centre was the United States working through the IMF, its currency the leading key currency, convertible into gold at the American Treasury. Exchange-rate changes of the major currencies were few; the rate for the American dollar was regarded as immutable as the nth currency upon which the (n-1) other cur-

---

[1] The references made here to Fund affairs over a period of ten or more years are necessarily truncated. Readers requiring amplification should consult the writer's *International Monetary Policy: Bretton Woods and After* (Macmillan, London, 1975) chs 5, 6 and 7.

rencies stabilised. Only in the absence of an adjustment mechanism was Bretton Woods not a gold standard. No recognised set of procedures corrected a deficit: each country was left to itself to achieve this when need arose, by *ad hoc* policies. The system was ended – by the inability of the United States to act as the centre country, to maintain a balance of payments appropriate to its key-currency role, and to achieve its own adjustment without a change of its own exchange rate. Moreover, by exporting its inflation to other nations it forced upon them policies which were inimical to the continuance of the system.

4

International Money

(i) Introduction

No set of problems is as central to the international monetary system as that which surrounds the use of international money itself. In the answers given to a set of questions concerning international money depends the whole stability and character of the system. The salient questions are three in number.

(1) What shall act as international money? An answer to this question must concern itself with how to establish the most widespread and complete acceptability of the money form.
(2) Who, or what institution, is to control the supply of international money; should that money, or some part of it, be established by international fiat?
(3) What shall determine the quantity and, above all, changes in the quantity of international money? This question requires an examination of the forces determining the demand and supply of international money and of the changes of these variables as time passes.

We justify this analysis in international money by the central role which it must play in balance-of-payments adjustment and therefore in the stability of the international economy as a whole. In face of a balance-of-payments disequilibrium – for example, a deficit – there are only four choices open to the country concerned: it may allow the deficit to continue meeting it by an outflow of its reserves of international money; it may deflate prices and income relative to other countries in the world system; it may devalue its exchange rate; or it may suppress the deficit by means of direct

51

controls on real or monetary .transactions. In the event of an international system in which exchange rates are to be fixed, the choices are cut to three, and if domestic macro-policies are to be aimed at high employment and growth, they reduce to two. It is evident that in circumstances where choices of adjustment methods are severely constrained, the size of the stock of international money becomes crucial – in the extreme case being the last defence of multilateral trade and convertible payments.

In this chapter we shall examine the three salient questions posed above regarding international money. What should it be? Who should control it? How should its quantity and distribution be influenced?

(ii) What is international money?

Of the three forms of international money – gold, key currencies, and the facilities of the IMF – we concern ourselves dominantly with the two latter. The claims of gold to be considered are slight, and in so far as they exist at all are based on historical arguments applicable to conditions which no longer exist. Gold has been demonetized by the IMF with the concurrence of leading central banks. It is highly unlikely that it will again play more than a peripheral role in the monetary system.[1] The case for including it is discussed later in this chapter.

From past history, present circumstances and future prospects it is key currencies which must be central to the total of international money. Supplementation of its amount by the creation of fiat

[1]If we accept the definition of the Group of Ten of international reserves as 'those assets of [a country's] monetary authorities that can be used directly, or through assured convertibility into other assets, to support its rate of exchange when its external payments are in deficit' (Ossola Report of Group of Ten, 1965, p. 21), we must exclude gold. It is not now used by national exchange funds for intervention in support of exchange funds, nor is it often exchanged into currencies for that purpose. Although central banks have large gold holdings they hold these rather as 'reserves for reserves' conscious of the fact that the wide fluctuations in price to which gold is subject render it undesirable to switch frequently from gold to currencies, or vice versa. The fact is that gold is now too illiquid to class as international liquidity.

money by the IMF may be extended but there is no immediate prospect of this superseding key currencies.

Any currency which is to serve satisfactorily as a reserve currency for other countries must clearly satisfy certain conditions. First, it must be the currency of a great trading nation, and one which may be earned easily by normal trade and whose balances carry the promise that they may be exchanged for goods both desirable in themselves and for the world demand which exists for them. Second, the currency must be stable in value, or, at least, in a world where currencies are losing value it must lose value no faster than other currencies. Third, it must be a currency which is supported in its home country by great and experienced banking institutions of skill and probity. And, finally, such a currency must be free from recurrent scarcity or glut. Of the currencies which have acted as international money, only sterling in the nineteenth century fully met this specification. The US dollar in the 1950s and 1960s did not, but it met it nearly enough to serve – albeit unsatisfactorily. Its shortcomings as a reserve currency were indeed highlighted by reference to these criteria. What the dollar did possess in this period and which enabled it to soldier on for so long, was confidence – confidence which derived initially in the 1950s from its great strength as a currency in the immediate post-war period and from the power and prestige of the United States. But neither the power of the currency nor the prestige of the country endured, and by the late 1960s the difficulties of the dollar as the centre currency of Bretton Woods were evident. Confidence in it was eroded and its central position became untenable.

So far, we have spoken of the world at large, but in a world of floating exchange rates, such as that which has existed since 1970 and in which a trend towards currency blocs has been observable, a number of key currencies may coexist, each serving as such within a group of countries. This has occurred either because the key currency has some vestigial primacy within the group – as with sterling within the remains of the sterling area, or the franc in the former French colonies – or because it is a trading and financial convenience to stabilise on the major vehicle currency of the trading bloc. Under such conditions where there are several key currencies rather than one, an element of instability arises if they are of varying strengths. Events deemed a threat to one currency by speculators may cause capital funds to migrate to others. There may be a condition of unease with several key currencies absent in the case of one strong reserve currency. This, in the worst case, may cause a weak currency area to resort to control of payments outside its area, resulting in fragmentation of what ideally would be a multilateral trading system.

It is tempting to ask whether a country should welcome the establishment of its currency as a key currency. Is such a condition one to be courted, an object of foreign economic policy? One thing is sure. The leading examples of key currencies fell into the condition by chance rather than design. Britain in the nineteenth century was, after 1850, the leading trading nation. Balances of her currency were held for trade. Her banking system was the most sophisticated in the world. Only towards the end of the century did it come to be realised that sterling filled a unique role. Later, after the Second World War, the United States also fell into the role unwittingly. Its dominant economic position from 1945 to 1955 and the scarcity of its currency caused almost all other countries to accumulate its currency both for transactions and for reserves. By 1959, when full convertibility of other IMF currencies into dollars was declared, the Bretton Woods system became a dollar/gold exchange standard, it was too late for the USA to draw back. The only case known to the writer of a country pursuing a determined policy as to the 'promotion' of its currency to key-currency status, has been a negative one. Germany, in the period of its greatest financial strength from 1951 and later in arrangements under the European Monetary Agreement, has steadfastly opposed any measures which would lead to the establishment of the Deutschmark as a major key currency. Indeed, most of the evidence of the twentieth century leads one to the view that first Britain and then the United States were anxious in their turn to divest themselves of the key-currency mantle.[1]

[1]Britain certainly followed policies in the 1920s which showed a desire to hold on to key-currency status. It is the writer's impression that, later, Britain willingly met key-currency responsibilities, avoiding, for example, frequent devaluations in the post Second World War period. Ultimately, in the later 1960s, it was clear that the key-currency role was officially regarded as too onerous for British economic resources. The declaration of a free exchange rate for sterling in June 1972 may be regarded as the point at which any claim to key-currency status for sterling was abandoned.

To return to the question of whether there is a balance of advantage one way or the other for a country in key-currency status, perhaps the best way to divest it of the confused thinking of the past is to list the advantages and disadvantages of the role as experience has revealed them. The advantages are three in number.

(1) A key-currency country will have whatever advantages may accrue to the leading country in international finance. Foremost among these is a strong bargaining position *vis-à-vis* other countries in financial matters.
(2) Invisible earnings accrue to the key-currency country from the use of its banking system and financial facilities.
(3) Within narrow limits a key-currency country can allow a deficit of its balance of payments to continue unchecked, since this allows working balances of its currency to accumulate abroad.

The disadvantages of key-currency-country status are also three in number.

(1) Since the key currency is a numeraire for all other currencies, the key-currency country cannot, in a deficit of the balance of payments, use devaluation of its currency as an adjustment weapon. It is, as the jargon goes, subject to the $(n-1)$ constraint.
(2) The monetary policies of the key-currency country may often be constrained by its status as such. Macro-policies in general must be slanted towards its external position rather than towards its domestic price and income equilibrium.
(3) The policies suitable for a key-currency country may conflict with other important aspects of policy. For example, overseas investment and development aid may have to be curtailed in the interests of a suitable balance of payments. Equally, industrial policies, where they bear upon exporting (or import-competing) industries, may be constrained.

In weighing the balance of advantage for the country whose currency has evolved to the key-currency status, it seems, at least to this writer, that the negative aspects predominate. The conflicts between internal and external equilibrium are bad enough for any country; where they are complicated by key-currency status some of them become insoluble. The brief history of the international economy demonstrates this for both sterling and the US dollar. It would seem that we are too prone to attach advantage to the running of a great currency, and to overlook, or at least to diminish, its responsibilities.

The second question we set ourselves was: who, or what, should control the supply of international money? – if that magnitude is indeed controllable. We have, at least by inference, had more than one answer to this question in the international monetary system as it has evolved. Under a gold-specie standard the answer is, of course, that the supply of international money consists of the world's surviving gold stock plus the augmentation coming from current mining and discoveries. This magnitude is under no control other than that of blind chance. During the nineteenth century the gold standard was amply furnished with a supply of the metal coming from a series of world discoveries, but the expansion of trade generated the continual fear that gold might ultimately come in short supply and the system break down for lack of it. Once key currencies came to form the dominant proportion of international money, however, the supply of such currencies depended on the size of the balance-of-payments deficit of the key-currency country. To this in the post Second World War world was added the drawings of member countries on the IMF. This was further augmented in the 1970s and 1980s by the issue by the Fund of Special Drawing Rights. Thus the present supply of international money is not under a single control, but is primarily the result of the balance of payments of the key-currency country, and secondarily of the Fund's view of how much the key-currency supply requires augmentation from its own resources. Since the balance-of-payments deficit of the key-currency country is determined by many forces, least of all by the requirements of the rest of the international economy for international money, only a small part (perhaps 10 per cent or more) of the total of international liquidity is consciously controllable by the IMF.

It might be desirable on grounds of mere tidiness and delight in system for system's sake, to have all international money variable in amount and under the direct control of an international body, but that is a condition only to be achieved if some created international money form, such as the SDR, were to increase in quantity, gain general acceptance and oust key currencies from use as reserves. In heaven, international monetary affairs will no doubt be so administered; on earth, things are likely to remain less ordered for some time.

(iii) Demand and supply

We must now turn to more theoretical matters and examine in turn the demand for and the supply of international money. Second-line international liquidity will be dealt with in a later chapter. For the present it is sufficient to say that the total of second-line international liquidity helps to determine the balances of payments (particularly on capital account) of countries in the world system. To that extent it is a secondary determinant of the world demand for international money.

In dealing with domestic money it has been the theoretical tradition to adopt a demand-and-supply analysis. It is a convenience to apply this method to international money. In domestic monetary theory the relation between the demand for money and its supply leads us to a monetary explanation of movements in the price level. In the case of international money, demand for and supply of international money will interact to identify the optimal level of international money in relation to whatever form of adjustment of balances of payments is in force, whether it be exchange-rate changes, willingness to alter levels of domestic prices and costs, or willingness to impose direct balance-of-payments controls of varying stringency.

First let us look at demand.[1] For the world as a whole, demand for international money is determined by:

(1) the necessity of countries to deal with short-term fluctuations in current account receipts and payments;
(2) the necessity for countries to 'buy time' in selecting policies for dealing with a current-account disequilibrium;
(3) the need for countries to meet speculative attacks on their currencies; and

[1]The demand for international money is well discussed in R. G. Lipsey and R. Clower, 'The Present State of International Liquidity Theory', *AER, Papers and Proceedings*, vol. 63, no. 2, May 1968.

(4) the necessity of countries to deal with short-term variations in capital-account items – in so far as these are not cushioned by second-line international liquidity.

We might array the main factors in a formal demand function

$$D_{L1} = f[\{\Sigma_{n-1} (B_1 - B_t)\}, V_1, L_2]$$

where D_{L1} is the world demand for first-line international liquidity, B_1 is the balance of regular transactions, B_t the balance of settling transactions, and the sum of $(B_1 - B_t)$ for the $n - 1$ countries of the world system is the total of residual balances requiring settlement. V is the total volume of world trade, and L_2 is the prevailing quantity of second-line international liquidity.

The sources of supply of international money are two:

(1) deficits in the balances of payments of key-currency countries; and
(2) the capacity of the international monetary system to create international monetary media – i.e. at present, drawing rights on the currency-holdings and SDRs of the IMF.

These may be stated as:

$$S_{L1} = f[\Sigma_n(B_1 - B_t),R]$$

where S_{L1} is the world supply of first-line international liquidity, B_1 is the balance of regular transactions, B_t, the balance of settling transactions, and the sum of $(B_1 - B_t)$ for the nth country (countries) of the world system is the total of deficits available for use by other countries as settlement and reserve balances. R is the amount of IMF monetary facilities.

What inferences may be drawn from the relations between total demand and supply for international money? We cannot, as in the case of domestic money, combine them in a theory of equilibrium price. Domestic money has a high and relatively stable transactions demand; international money has a low transactions demand and is held for dominantly precautionary and speculative reasons. There is no meaningful concept of international price level.

We can, however, wring some significant conclusions from the analysis. Apart from arraying in an orderly fashion the main variables affecting the position of international liquidity, a comparison of demand and supply invites comparison of the magnitudes and the implications of excess of one over the other. The demand/supply approach demonstrates that there is some optimum level of reserves which satisfies the system. This optimum invites a dual approach. We may approach it qualitatively, arguing that it is a level (and distribution) of reserves sufficient that policies of control for single economies, such as those for preservation of employment or control of inflation, are not prejudiced by the condition and prospects of the balance of payments. Alternatively we may approach optimality of reserves quantitatively, looking for some objective statistical measure of reserve adequacy, or, even more ambitiously, of reserve optimality.

Look at some of the qualitative aspects of reserve optimality. If the demand for first-line international liquidity in the international economy exceeds supply, then countries with balance-of-payments deficits will, in default of adequate reserves, have to take action to adjust their deficits. If exchange rates are flexible, then depreciation of the rate may be sufficient to achieve the adjustment. If, however, exchange rates are fixed, then deficit countries will have either to deflate purposively their domestic levels of prices and income or resort to direct controls to suppress their deficits. In a fixed-exchange-rate world we may, therefore, expect a shortage of international liquidity to generate (a) a general deflationary tendency and/or (b) a propensity for trade to be constrained by direct government controls. In the opposite case, when the world stock of international liquidity exceeds demand, there is less necessity for immediate adjustment of balances of payments. Even if exchange rates are fixed, *a fortiori* if they are flexible, a deficit may be tolerated and met out of reserves. It is, for example, possible for a country running an external deficit as a result of domestic inflation to allow the inflation to go further and continue longer than would be the case if reserves were in short supply. A special case is that of a key-currency country which, if it incurs an external deficit due to domestic inflation, may finance the deficit by the build-up abroad of balances of its own currency. There is no sanction against the continuing deficit of the key-currency country unless the size and duration of its deficit invokes a confidence problem and threatens the status of the key currency. In the late 1960s and in the 1970s the United States followed this pattern, allowing its inflation to go unchecked, causing secondary inflationary effects on other trading countries.

What the demand/supply approach to the international liquidity problem reveals clearly is the significance of the adjustment mechanism in deciding the adequacy or otherwise of the world stock of international liquidity. The more smoothly the adjustment mechanism works, the lower the optimum level of first-line international liquidity needs to be.[1] This point can be quickly demonstrated in a conventional demand/supply diagram. Figure 4.1 depicts a conceptual market for international reserves. The X axis OX measures the quantity of international reserves in any time-period: on OY is measured the flexibility of the adjustment system, typified in this case by the degree of flexibility of the exchange rate.[2] In this diagram, DD, the demand curve for international reserves, is negatively sloped, no reserves being required when the exchange rate, at Y, is infinitely variable, maximum reserves being required when the exchange rate is fixed at X. The supply curve SS may be variously drawn. Under a pure gold standard, in the short term, the supply of international reserves is the existing world gold stock, and SS is vertical at that quantity. If one conceives first-line liquidity as consisting only of key currencies, then the supply curve is negatively sloped (as shown), for the supply of such currencies is greatest when key-currency countries do not correct their balance-of-payments deficits, as would be the case when exchange flexibility was low. Aggregate world reserves optimum to the given demand and supply of international liquidity would with these demand and supply functions be determined by their intersection at X.

[1]Assuming other features, such as desired levels of employment and income, remain constant.

[2]We might equally measure along OY some imaginary index of the propensity to impose direct controls on trade or an index of willingness to vary domestic income and prices. Neither of such variables is capable of being other than conceptual and their quantification is obviously not possible. Even an 'index of exchange stability' may be questionable, but at least on a comparative scale exchange stability can range from the fixed exchange rate, for years, to the freely floating exchange rate. One may grade between these extremes according to a 'frequency of allowable variation' scale.

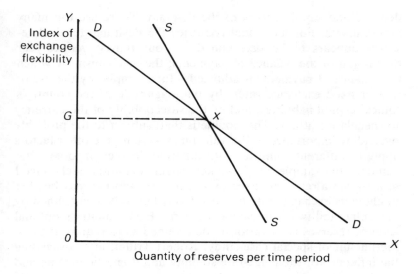

Figure 4.1

Changes in the *ceteris paribus* conditions, such as (a) increased willingness to vary prices and income and/or (b) increased willingness to resort to direct balance-of-payments controls, would shift *DD* to the left and lower the required quantity of reserves.

The implications of this diagram are necessarily simple when drawn from such a crude apparatus, but they are none the less significant. Any given level of demand for world reserves associated with a supply independently determined by the deficits of key-currency countries, generates a need for a given optimal quantity of reserves. This optimum level of reserves is associated with a condition of exchange stability as a vehicle of adjustment.

What of the second aspect of reserve optimality – quantification? In any problem that is of operational significance, as that of optimum reserve levels certainly is, it is tempting to try to compute a statistical measure of reserve adequacy. If we attempt to do this for the international economy as a whole we are faced with an intractable problem. The quantity of reserves will not only be determined by the adjustment system with which it is associated, but will change for all *ceteris paribus* changes which move the demand and supply curves of the diagram. There are too many determinants. For individual countries the desirable level of reserves appears to be determined by four things: year-to-year fluctuation of the balance of payments; the mechanism by which the balance of payments is adjusted – for example, by the use of free or fixed exchange rates; by the magnitude of the country's 'quick' capital liabilities; and by the susceptibility of the currency to speculative attack. The trouble is that, subject to the probably overriding importance of the adjustment system, the other factors apply to different countries with different degrees of force. One country, for example, may, as a key-currency country, feel obliged to maintain a relatively fixed exchange rate, another may be able to allow its exchange rate to move freely but to be constrained by the vulnerability of its capital account. Each country's optimal level of reserves is so variously determined as to require it to be the pursuit of special case-study. Robert Triffin, after discussing the influence of exchange-rate stability and domestic income and employment policies on the desirable level of reserves, summarises the issue as follows:

> These considerations do not lend themselves to any scientific determination of 'ideal' level of reserves either for an individual country or for the world at large. There is certainly a very wide range of actual reserve levels that might be regarded as satisfactory or acceptable, by the monetary authorities and that would not induce them to modify their policies in such a way as to sacrifice other and more fundamental policy goals, such as desirable rates of employment and economic growth, price stability, and so on.[1]

If we turn to historical data and try to connect totals of world reserves to trade volume, the associations are not very helpful. First, trade volume is not the sole determinant of the need for reserves; rather it is instability of the balance of payments at any trade volume that is important. But since we have figures for the former but not for the latter, we make use of them, taking refuge in the possibility that large instability may correlate with large

[1]Robert Triffin, *Our International Monetary System; Yesterday, To-day and To-morrow* (Yale University Press, 1968) p. 89.

trade volume, which may not be the case. Moreover, we do not know whether in any past period international liquidity was adequate or not. It may have been regarded as so, but absence of complaint in the contemporary literature cannot be taken as a reliable indicator of adequacy. In not many past periods were we as sensitive to the international liquidity problem as we have been since the Second World War.

Thus far in our discussion of international money we have been concerned with its functions and the demand for it which results from these. We now turn to supply, considering in turn the three elements of which international money is composed: gold, key currencies and the facilities of the IMF. There is immediately some doubt as to whether gold should be included in this list. It no longer fulfils completely the functions of an international commodity money. The severance in 1971 of the link provided by a fixed price between the US dollar and gold, destroyed the gold-exchange standard which by 1971 Bretton Woods had become. The IMF through its Interim Committee in January 1976 took steps to change the role of gold in the IMF and in the world system which aimed at ultimate demonetisation of the metal. These steps, combined with the practices of central banks in their usages with regard to gold holding for reserves, leave us at present in a transitional stage. Gold is not yet demonetised. It plays a vestigial role. Moreover, the speculative demand for it combined with the conventional view of the superiority of a commodity money may yet ensure it some part in events.

The *International Financial Statistics* manual published by the IMF includes gold (valued at 35 SDR per ounce) under the rubric of Total Reserves. In spite of the measures taken in the last decade to demonetise gold it is realistic to assume that, in extremity, gold-holding central banks would use their gold holdings to support their currencies. Indeed, it would be more realistic to include gold at a higher valuation since gold sales to support a currency are likely to be made at the world market price. In any event two facts emerge from the IFS table: the dominance of key-currency holdings, and the relatively small contribution of Fund-created assets (15 percent). We are still far away from a situation in which world money consists of directly created assets of a central agency.

The total world stock of international money can be easily

calculated from published statistics.[1] In general terms it consists of (i) the total stock of monetary gold already held by monetary authorities plus the flow per year coming from world production, less the use of gold for industrial purposes, less the drain of monetary gold into private hoards held for speculative purposes; (ii) stocks of key currencies held by monetary authorities for exchange reserves, plus the balance-of-payments deficits of key-currency countries; and (iii) the total unused drawing rights of IMF member countries upon the Fund, plus the uncommitted part of their SDR allocations. Table 4.1 shows the first-line international liquidity, including and excluding monetary gold, at year-ends 1978 and 1980 and at February 1986.

(iv) Are SDRs the answer?

It is to the SDR that we naturally turn for hope of establishing a really flexible and controlled form of international money.[2] The SDR scheme has been in operation for sixteen years and has had only limited success. What are its limitations?

Born in 1967 with the Rio de Janeiro Agreement, the creation of SDRs dichotomised the Fund's contribution to international liquidity. First, there is the General Account of the Fund through which all its business in national currencies is conducted. This reflects the currency holdings coming from its members' quota contributions and the purchase and sale of these currencies under the arrangements in force since the Fund's inception. The available currencies may be further increased by the Fund's entitlement to borrow currencies from its ten leading members under the so-called GAB arrangement of 1962.[3] Second, there is the Special Drawing Account through which all operations and transactions in

---

[1] For example, *International Financial Statistics* (IMF, Washington) publish in their monthly edition figures for world and country holdings of gold, foreign exchange reserves, and SDR and reserve positions in the IMF.

[2] Growth of available Fund resources other than SDRs must depend almost entirely on expansion of Fund quotas and Fund ability to borrow from member countries.

[3] By the General Arrangements to Borrow, the Fund may borrow up to $6 billion from its ten richest members – the so-called Group of Ten.

Table 4.1 Composition of official holdings of reserve assets, all countries (selected recent years) (billion SDRs)

	1978	1980	1986
Gold (valued at London Market price)	179.9	440.2	277.7
	(42%)	(58%)*	(43%)
Foreign exchange	224.2	293.1	329.8
	(53%)	(38%)	(51%)
Fund related assets:			
Reserve positions in the Fund	14.8	16.8	18.5
SDRs	8.1	11.8	21.4
	(5%)	(4%)	(6%)
Total reserves	427.0	761.9	647.5
Ratio of non-gold reserves to world imports (year ends)	22.9%	20.9%	—

*Sharp fluctuations in the relative importance of official gold holdings as part of total reserves are due to fluctuations in the market price of gold. Gold holdings, both as to total and country distribution, have been stable since 1973.

SOURCES: *Annual Report* of IMF, 1984; IMF, *IFS*.

SDRs are conducted. The SDR is essentially only an entry in this account at the Fund. Moreover, it is an asset which may be held only by (a) national monetary authorities (who must be members of the Fund) and (b) the General Account of the Fund to which participant countries are permitted to transfer SDRs for certain specified purposes.[1] It is apparent that the SDR is a created deposit of a member with the Fund – created in the sense that it is an overdraft unit issued by the Fund, drawing its credit-standing from the fact that it confers on the holder the right to obtain its defined equivalent in foreign exchange from other Fund members and/or that it discharges specified obligations of members towards the Fund's General Account. For the first time in currency history an international organisation has been given power to create international fiat money. Conscious of this innovation and of the lofty purposes of such creation, the Fund Agreement waxes almost lyrical when it states that 'the Fund shall seek to meet the long-

[1] For example, to pay charges levied by the Fund or to repay drawings from the General Account.

term global need . . . to supplement existing reserves . . . and . . . avoid economic stagnation and deflation as well as excess demand and inflation in the world'.[1]

Conditions surround the decision of the Fund to create and allocate SDRs:

(a) The decision must be voted upon by the governors of the Fund and must carry an 85 per cent majority of total voting power.
(b) The decision must cater to a global need and not to the need of a specific country or countries.
(c) The need for supplementation must be a long-term need.
(d) the allocation must further the Fund's general aims of expanding trade, securing exchange stability and orderly exchange adjustment.

Six SDR allocations have so far been made by the fund: $9.4 billion in three allocations in 1970, 1971 and 1972; and SDRs 12 billion in three allocations in 1979, 1980 and 1981; a total of SDRs 21.4 billion.[2]

SDRs can be used for a variety of transactions and operations, including the acquisition of other Fund members' currencies, settlement of financial obligations and the making of loans. They may be used in swap arrangements and as security for financial obligations. Thus some countries may accumulate SDRs in excess of their total cumulative allocations while some may (by the same amount collectively) fall short of their original allocation. The first group are paid interest on their excess SDRs, the second group pay interest to the Fund on their total used SDRs. To avoid all the SDRs in existence flowing to surplus countries there is a prescribed limit beyond which such countries are not obliged to accept SDRs. Equally there is a minimum below which the SDR holdings of countries may not, on the average, fall. If a country's holdings of SDRs fall below the average it is required to reconstitute them by purchase.

The SDR scheme is simple and adaptable. It is less complex than the elaborate accounting scheme involved in EPU units in the

[1]Article XXIV, Sec. 1(a).

[2]The value of the SDR was, until 1971, equal to one dollar US. Thereafter the value of the SDR varied proportionately to a basket of sixteen currencies.

European Payments Union between 1950 and 1959, less flexible than the 1942 Keynes Plan for an International Clearing Union which it resembles in several respects. Given favourable conditions it should be capable of smooth operation and expansion. Why, then, has it had such limited success? The first reason is that it was set in motion at an inopportune time. In 1970–72 the US deficit was at its height and the dollar reserves of countries were being amply supplied by the deficit. The Nixon measures of 1971 threw the whole Bretton Woods system into confusion; 1972 and 1973 were spent in trying to negotiate a new parity for the dollar through the Smithsonian and Paris Agreements. International monetary reform was attempted in 1972–3, and failed. The oil crisis of 1974 followed. From then forward the world was awash in petro-dollars. The enormous increase in foreign-exchange holdings as reserves swamped the modest increase in SDRs, and ensured the continuance of the world on a dollar standard determined by the balance of payments of the United States. The second reason for the limited use of SDRs has been the qualified acceptance of countries to make use of them. Surplus countries questioned the utility of accumulating them. Third, there was a difficulty with their creation in that the Third World lobby in the Fund wished to link their creation with the wider problem of development. Instead of distributing them to members in proportion to members' quotas, it was demanded that they be issued to Third World countries in balance-of-payments difficulties, which might then use them to cover their deficits. This 'Link' Plan was not to the liking of the rich industrial countries, and other things being what they were it seemed better to hold further creations in abeyance – this being easily accomplished in that decisions to create SDRs require an 85 per cent majority of member votes. Finally, the United States by its large voting power in the Fund has been able at will to block, when necessary, further issues of SDRs. All in all, politics and economics have not been kind to the SDR scheme, although the mechanism as such has much to commend it.

It is appropriate to end this chapter by exploring, very briefly, the way in which international reserves might be adjusted in the future. For this purpose we may make the following assumptions. First, with any given adjustment system, reserves are likely to be demand-determined – that is, that the supply curve of reserves shown in Figure 4.1 is vertical at whatever quantity of reserves for the moment exists. Second, while some additional reserves may be forthcoming from the deficits of key-currency countries, these may be accounted as windfall gains to the total (causing the *SS* curve to have negative slope) and justifying downward adjustment of the total reserves to be created. Finally, expansion of international reserves over time might be achieved by successive (preferably annual) allocations of SDRs, thus causing the SDR component of total reserves to grow relatively as well as absolutely.

In the light of these assumptions the size of future SDR allocations should be determined as follows. Reserves should grow *pari passu* with the growth of trade. To the trend growth of GNP of countries in total[1] might be applied the functional relation between income and trade growth rates. The result might typically be a trend rate of growth of world trade volume of 4 per cent.[2]

It has been estimated[3] that the income elasticity of the real demand for reserves is 0.65, which would generate a growth in the real demand for reserves of just over 2.5 per cent per year – an SDR creation of 9 billion.

This figure, however, requires certain adjustments. First, account should be taken of the very low level of reserves of certain developing countries. Here, two approaches are possible. One approach would be to take the last date of the country receiving an SDR allocation, probably January 1981, and start the allocation of SDRs from there. Unfortunately this would probably result in inequity, in that all countries would then claim this privilege. More satisfactory would be to agree a safe level of reserves, expressed as a percentage of imports.[4] To the extent that existing reserves fell short of this datum the shortfall should be added to the country's allocation. This principle applied to a number of aid-receiving Third World countries would considerably increase the SDR 9

[1]GNP growth of OECD countries would be a useful indicator.

[2]J. D. Williamson, assessing the case for a new SDR allocation, takes 4 per cent as his trend figure for world trade growth: J. D. Williamson, 'International Liquidity', in *The International Monetary System, Forty Years After Bretton Woods* (Federal Reserve Bank of Boston, 1984), p. 66.

[3]G. M. von Furstenberg, 'New Estimates of the Demand for Non-Gold Reserves under Floating Exchange Rates', *Journal of International Money and Finance*, 1982, p. 88.

[4]It was often argued that, under Bretton Woods conditions, a minimum safe ratio of reserves to imports would be 25 per cent – or reserves equal to three months' imports.

billion figure given above. It would, however, be a once-over increase to be followed in subsequent years only by the amount appropriate to the annual trade growth.

Finally, the annual allocation on a trade growth basis could be reduced by any positive increase in other reserve assets such as key currencies over the period. Thus the role of SDRs would continue to be that of the residual in keeping reserve growth in step with the growth of trade, but, in the long run, world stock of SDRs would be greatly increased and, it might be hoped, their role universally accepted.

The political feasibility of even such a simple annual augmentation of reserves is at the moment very questionable. The United States opposes further allocations of SDRs for the moment, and other countries join in opposition for a variety of reasons. Such a variously motivated constituency of opposition demonstrates that it will take some time for SDR allocation on an automatic basis to win acceptance. We end this chapter, perhaps on a negative note, by summarising briefly the main objections made by the opponents of SDR allocation.

First, we must distinguish between more or less *ad hoc* objections peculiar to current circumstances and more deep-seated misgivings arising from doubts as to the SDR scheme *per se*. Two main *ad hoc* objections are made. The first is that augmentation of reserves at the present juncture would be inflationary, an understandable fear at a time when the inflationary levels of the 1970s are only just coming under control. The second is that an SDR allocation might weaken the resolve of debtor countries to undertake the adjustment of their balances of payments, which is a necessary stage in solving the debt problem. This is a wider issue but it should be noted that the orders of magnitude do not do much to support the argument. The larger debtors – for example, Brazil, Mexico, Poland – measure their debt liabilities in many billions, whereas an SDR allocation measured in the way described above would fall far short of SDR 1 billion for such countries.

The *ad hoc* objections will no doubt always exist in some form or other, and their pacification must be left to negotiators of the time. It is from the deep-seated doubts which have always surrounded the SDR scheme that we are likely to learn its weaknesses. The deeper suspicions which surround the SDR scheme can be summarised in four words: inflation, seigniorage, aid, and confidence.

As long as the international liquidity problem has existed the objection that expansion of the international liquidity stock would lead to inflation, perhaps on a world scale, has been made. It is a survival of the old monetary-base approach to reserves, coming down to us from gold-standard times and superseded in the 1950s by the so-called buffer-stock view. In an age when reserves are divorced from the domestic money stock the objection has little validity. A country does not now expand its money supply directly or on a fractional relation with its reserves. In one sense, however, the objection has weight. A country which has created a deficit in its balance of payments by over-expansion of its domestic economy, and which would, in the absence of adequate reserves, be forced to take action to adjust the deficit, might well, having larger reserve holdings, allow inflation and the deficit to continue while exporting the inflation to other countries. One may certainly argue that high reserve levels may erode the will to preserve balance-of-payments equilibrium.

Seigniorage is an interesting but not a compelling argument against creation of any form of world money. Who is to get the resources that accrue with the free issue of SDRs to members of the Fund? The answer is that thus far these benefits have been distributed to members, as are the SDRs themselves, pro rata, with the size of quotas. Since quotas are largest for major industrial countries, smallest for poor developing countries, the allocation process so far as seigniorage is concerned is a case of 'To them that hath shall be given'. It is neither economically unsound nor ethically repugnant to this writer that the developing countries should be the major rather than the minor recipients of this not very large allocation.

If we accept the seigniorage distribution advocated in the previous paragraph we accept its corollary – that SDR allocations have in them an implicit element of economic aid. This is acceptable to this writer, to supporters of economic aid in general, and of course to the developing countries themselves; but to a number of the Group of Ten countries there is a qualified acceptance of the aid principle, a belief that aid should be given to selected countries and not distributed widely, a belief that aid should be tied so as to benefit the donor as well as the recipient, or a belief, appropriate to tidy minds, that the Fund is not an aid-dispensing institution. For whatever reasons aid in the form of SDR allocations may be opposed, that opposition must be recognised as retarding the increasing use of this reserve asset.

Finally, confidence, a *sine qua non* of the success of all money forms, is essential to the SDR in greater measure than it at present possesses. We have overestimated the sophistication of international bankers and central banks. We have assumed the transition from monetary-based reserves to unbacked, created reserves to have been smoothly and completely made. If this *were* so, it should be a matter of indifference to central banks in which asset – gold, currencies or SDRs – they hold their reserves. In fact it is *not* so. Switching between asset forms within the general category of reserves may be perilous. How perilous is largely irrelevant: the fact that central bankers regard it as perilous is the important fact. This is evident in the case of gold, once the bedrock of central-bank reserves. Now subject to wide price fluctuations, its conversion into currencies, which is necessary for intervention purposes, carries a large risk element, so that gold has been derogated to a background, last-ditch role as a reserve asset. The fact that reserves exist for currency intervention to support an exchange rate, places a heavy preference on currencies as reserve assets. These are immediately usable for intervention. Gold or SDRs (or other Fund-created assets) have to be converted into currencies. At the least this is an inconvenience, at the most it is a deterrent because of possible loss in the switch.

There is no doubt that the fact that the SDR is a 'holding' asset, not capable of being directly used for intervention, dooms it to the status of second-class citizen among reserve assets. At the moment, SDRs have to be exchanged for currencies within the Fund and with the Fund's co-operation. At best this is an impedance. For some countries the thought occurs that the US-dominated Fund may not always be co-operative. It has been argued that were the SDR a widely used form of paper, usable in the private sector, having a large market and moving smoothly and easily between private and official sectors, it would be held with more confidence as a reserve asset. This condition lies in the future. In the meantime the SDR is used with some qualifications by Fund members. Automatically increasing, unbacked international money is further away, even now, than those who hailed the Rio Agreement in 1967 then imagined.

5

What Sort of Exchange Rates?

(i) Introduction

No question is so important, so divisive and so perennial as the title of this chapter. Conventional wisdom in different periods has given various answers. The original simple categories supported by the antagonists of 'fixed' or 'floating' have been expanded by debate, taxonomy and nuance of meaning to a long list of alternative exchange-rate behaviour patterns on a spectrum between the two extremes.[1] The final conclusions of one age are superseded as change occurs in international relations, structures and strengths and makes new judgements necessary. There is no final condition of best balance of advantage.

We will confine our attention in this chapter to two actual exchange-rate systems, whose usages span the past forty years: the adjustable-peg system of Bretton Woods, and the flexible-rate pattern which succeeded it in 1971–3. The Bretton Woods system was near to that of fixed rates. Each currency in the IMF defined its unit in terms of the US dollar, thus defining its rate in terms of every other. These parities were only alterable on proof of a so-called 'fundamental disequilibrium' in the balance of payments. The quarter-century of Bretton Woods saw over a hundred devaluations and only four revaluations in an upward direction. The flexible-rate system under which we now exist began with the breakup of the Bretton Woods system in 1971. Canada floated her

---

[1]The author finds that in an earlier book he distinguished three sets of possible exchange-rate patterns and seven sub-sets: *International Monetary Policy. Bretton Woods and After* (London, Macmillan, 1975) p. 78.

currency in June 1970, sterling in June 1972, Japan and Italy in February 1973, and the United States and the countries of the European Snake in March 1973. Thereafter, countries managed their floats variously. At the end of 1983, 36 countries pegged their currencies to the US dollar, 13 to the French franc, 5 to other currencies, 12 to the SDR, 33 according to a set of indicators, 8 under co-operative exchange arrangements and 38 under a variety of other arrangements. This could scarcely be described as an exchange-rate system – rather it reflected a variety of views as to how best the exchange rate could be managed and where national best interests lay.

The adjustable-peg system served the Bretton Woods system during a period of great international trade expansion and, at first blush, imparted to that system a desirable element of stability. Yet almost from the outset of Bretton Woods, and certainly during the period when it was functioning at its fullest, the adjustable-peg arrangements were under strain and were the subject of criticism particularly by advocates of more-flexible rates. With the passing of Bretton Woods something of that flexibility was achieved, at least in the sense that rate changes were made more often, that they were made both upwards and downwards and that attempts were made to allow the exchange rate to act as an adjuster of the balance of payments. Yet a period which includes in its events two major energy crises, a surge of worldwide inflation and two world recessions, one of them the deepest since the 1930s, necessarily placed great strains on exchange rates, and their management and role has been called in question. There has been since the late 1970s some nostalgia for the stable rates of Bretton Woods but also a realisation that such a state could not function well in present world conditions.

In this chapter, we shall attempt to dredge from all this what wisdom we may. First we shall take a brief look at the adjustable-peg system and the criticism it invoked. Then we shall turn to the question of what became of the high hopes of its critics and how their systems fared in the fast-running tides of the 1970s.

(ii) The adjustable-peg system and its critics

The planners of the post-war monetary system in 1942–4 were adversely influenced by two features of the inter-war payments system and sought to avoid them: the disadvantages of the old gold standard, which required countries to subjugate domestic-policy objectives to control of the balance of payments; and the believed disadvantages of fluctuating exchange rates, in particular competitive depreciation. They sought to embody in the post-war system the advantages of previous systems without incurring the disadvantages of either. The resulting compromise system, referred to at the time as one of 'managed flexibility', proved anything but flexible in practice, and its baptismal name soon fell out of use, being replaced by the name 'adjustable peg'.

The system required individual countries to stabilise their domestic economies at full employment and to adjust their balances of payments by infrequent discrete changes in otherwise fixed exchange rates. It was assumed that changes of exchange rate are made only to meet structural changes in a country's foreign trade position, and that short-term variations in the external balance may be handled by reserve transfers. It was the practice to define each currency unit in terms of a numeraire and to allow a narrow band of allowable fluctuation around the central exchange rate.[1] This was vestigial of the gold standard when the gold points, and/or a gap between a central bank's buying and selling prices for gold, determined the width of the band, but it had utility even in a non-gold-based system since such a band enabled day-to-day and hour-by-hour fluctuations in the rate to be accommodated in what was still a virtually fixed-rate system. To maintain a single defined rate with no fluctuation would have involved an intolerable amount of central-bank participation in the market and would indeed have been near to impossible.

When the monetary authority of any country wanted to alter its exchange rate it had only to alter the parity of its monetary unit with the numeraire. Thus if X lowered the price of gold by 10 per cent in terms of its own currency (assuming gold to be the numeraire) it thereby appreciated its exchange by 11 per cent in terms of every other currency whose gold price remained unaltered. Thus, under the adjustable-peg system, the change of rate was made by the monetary authority as a deliberate act to achieve adjustment, and was of such magnitude as would, in its judgement, serve to restore equilibrium.

---

[1] This band was ± 1 percent from 1946 to 1971. In the latter year it was altered, under the Smithsonian Agreement, to ± 2.25 per cent.

What principles were implicit in the adjustable-peg system? Perhaps the most apparent was that it saw disequilibrium in the balance of payments as being located in the current account and as being correctable by an exchange-rate change. A second principle was that of rejection of the method of adjusting the balance of payments by domestic income changes. The exchange rate and not domestic income was seen as the primary vehicle of adjustment. Both of these principles were abrogated in practice. Disequilibria during the 1946–71 period were prominently (although not entirely) in the capital account, while the amount of international reserves, particularly after 1960, was insufficient to permit the exchange rate to be the sole engine of balance-of-payments adjustment.

Apart from these basic principles there were a host of secondary implications. The system raised the whole question of who was to manage, time and co-ordinate changes of exchange rates: what should be the magnitude of changes and what should be the criteria of deciding when they should be made. In the original Bretton Woods conception, the IMF was, somewhat nebulously, seen as sharing responsibility for these decisions with sovereign governments. It did not take long to learn that next to foreign policy and defence policy there is no field which governments regard as so sacred to their sole power as that of exchange rates. Apart from all this, the adjustable-peg system, particularly as it was seen by the IMF and as the Fund sought to administer it, carried the implication, only vaguely sensed in 1944, that frequency of changes of exchange rates is related to the world stock and distribution of international liquidity, indeed that it is only possible to decide upon any particular system of exchange rates in the light of the size of that stock.

Were the adjustable-peg system merely a figment of the historical past we might dismiss it, but it is now (1986) beginning to invoke in accredited observers of the international scene a dangerous nostalgia which may result in its later promotion to a viable alternative to the present exchange-rate pattern of flexible rates.[1]

---

[1] The following is fairly typical; 'an increasing number of participants in the international markets for money and goods, after living with the resulting non-system of floating exchange rates for over a decade, are beginning to yearn for the comparative orderliness and stability which their idealised memories associate with "the days of Bretton Woods" ': Robert V. Roosa, 'Exchange Rate Arrangements in the Eighties', in *The International Monetary System*, Reserve Bank of Boston, Conference Series No. 28, May 1984, p. 104.

For this reason, if for no other, it is necessary to examine it more closely.

Suppose a country under the adjustable-peg system of the 1960s incurred a deficit in its balance of payments. Its exchange rate then depreciated under the influence of excess of its currency on the foreign exchange market and, if the deficit was large enough, it depreciated to the lower level of the allowable range of 1 per cent above and below parity. At the lower support point the deficit-country's exchange fund would buy, with its foreign currency reserves, all further excess offers of its currency. If the deficit was brief, the country would incur only a small fall in its reserves, but if it was of long duration the drain on its reserves would be large and the deficit country might be driven to borrow from the IMF or seek a stabilisation loan abroad in either the public or private sectors. If the deficit still persisted, the country would be forced to devalue its currency. Whatever the time-span of such events, their sequence would be clear and recognisable, inviting speculation against the currency. This speculation would benefit the speculators if the devaluation took place, and would not penalise them[1] if it did not, thus providing an attractive one-way option the effect of which would be to add disequilibrium in the capital account to the original disequilibrium in the current account.

Even if we set aside the speculation effect of the adjustable peg, it had other deficiencies. Any adjustment system should have its own corrective to imbalance, so, we may ask, what adjustment forces had the adjustable peg? The short answer is: very inadequate forces. There would be some adjustment coming from income changes. Domestic income would fall with the deficit causing some fall in imports. But income changes will never completely adjust a payments deficit[2] and monetary forces may be slow to complete the process. To the extent that the deficit causes residents to reduce their cash balances as payments in domestic money are transferred abroad, and assuming that the monetary authority pursues a passive policy, domestic cash balances are reduced. Once these balances reach the minimum that the community are prepared to hold, a rise in the rate of interest will take

---

[1] Except to the extent of small transfer costs in the exchange market.

[2] For amplification of this assertion, see W. M. Scammell, *International Trade and Payments* (London, Macmillan, 1974) pp. 339–40.

place which improves the deficit by two routes: by the deflationary effect of the higher interest rate upon investment, and by short-term capital being drawn to the country by higher yield. It is doubtful, however, whether these adjustment effects would be strong enough or swift enough to correct the balance of payments before the deficit country's reserves were depleted. Apart from the slowness of the monetary adjustment, its efficacy rests upon the assumption of no change in the money supply by the central bank. This is unlikely: it is far more probable that fear of unemployment as a result of rising interest rates would lead the central bank to ease the money supply in order to hold interest rates at their existing level. One is forced to the conclusion that in any practical time-period relevant to short-run adjustment, there is no system of adjustment under the adjustable peg.

The adjustable peg was probably the most criticised facet of the Bretton Woods system. From the early 1950s the system was under increasing attack from many economists, who advocated free-exchange-rate systems of various degrees of liberality. From the mid-1960s the Fund was under criticism for attempting to transform the Bretton Woods system to one of virtually fixed exchange rates.

There were two stages in the controversy which led to the discarding of the adjustable peg and the adoption of flexible rates. First, there were the objections to the adjustable peg itself – the encouragement of speculation, the lack of an adequate adjustment system, the question of who was to manage exchange rates and according to what criteria were rate changes to be made. Then there was a second stage: the claim that flexible rates would provide in themselves a superior exchange-rate pattern. Such a claim was made on several grounds and by diverse groups. The claims were simple. Free rates was the method of the market. The exchange rate is of all the macro variables the easiest to alter, so why not leave it to the forces of the market to adjust the exchange rate and the balance of payments. In the market for foreign exchange there would always be some rate at which demand for and supply of a currency would balance. The lack of an adjustment system, which was the great fault of the adjustable peg, would be met by a free exchange market. Moreover, in a full-employment Keynesian world what could be more appropriate than to regulate the domestic economy for high growth and employment and leave the balance of payments to the exchange rate and the forces of the market. The interdependence of the external and internal equilibria of the economy was ignored.[1] The more obvious drawbacks of free rates – uncertainty, slowness in adjustment because of the J-curve effect, susceptibility to governmental manipulation – were either ignored or made light of.

Despite criticism the adjustable peg was a good survivor. Although attacked by academic economists it was supported by the financial establishment of bankers, central bankers and politicians. Uncertainty frightened them. Might free rates not be inflationary? Moreover, by the 1960s there were few practising bankers around who had operated in the free-exchange-rate milieu of the 1930s, and what they heard of that condition did not encourage them. A generation bred on certainty, at least in the exchange market, was in the saddle. It took major events to break up the Bretton Woods system and present the new generation with no alternative but free rates to effect the change.

While this intellectual debate was unfolding the adjustable peg was acquiring a record – of exactly twenty-five years – by which it should certainly be judged. The salient features of this record must be kept in mind. They are worth more than twenty years of academic argument. First, while the adjustable-peg system was in operation from 1946 to 1971, for more than half that time it was bolstered by support programmes and protected by exchange controls. From 1946 until January 1959 it was really a hybrid system in which exchange rates were supported by large stabilisation loans, by the European Recovery Programme and by regional payments arrangements such as the European Payments Union. All the major countries, except the United States, operated systems of control over trade and payments. Not until 1959 when the Western European currencies were made fully convertible into dollars was the Bretton Woods system free to operate as

---

[1]Supporters of free exchange rates at this period were peculiarly blind on this interdependence. After all, IS/LM analysis was already widely taught and accepted. There was ample theory already in existence to warn economists that the exchange rate could not be regarded *in vacuo*. It seems that it needed the experience of a decade of fluctuating rates to convince economists that the macro-stabilisation problem is more complex than they assumed it to be.

its architects had intended. By 1968 it was exhibiting such strain as to create new control systems, directed against the gold market and capital movements, to support it. The adjustable-peg system can be said to have survived the first dollar problem (1945–55) by expedients, controls and interventions, and to have perished in the second dollar problem in spite of controls and interventions. In its pure essence it existed only between 1959 and 1968. Judgements on its efficiency must be based on a far narrower time-span than at first appears.

The second feature of interest in the record was the need, predictable on theoretical grounds, for a large and well-distributed stock of international liquidity. This requirement was the result not only of a system of virtually fixed exchange rates, but also of the fact that reserves were dominantly held in the form of key currencies, the US dollar and the pound, and that each of these currencies was inhibited in efficiency by its own peculiar problems. The Bretton Woods system was ultimately destroyed by this fact. To put the point in another way, the slowness of governments and monetary authorities to perceive the weaknesses of key currencies and to proceed with the technical task of providing an international credit unit, left a basically simple dilemma: there was not sufficient acceptable international liquidity to maintain the type of exchange-rate system which the IMF and the central bankers appeared to want.

The third feature which emerges from the record is the way in which during its life the image of the adjustable peg changed. By the founding fathers of Bretton Woods it was seen as a condition under which exchange rates would change from time to time, in which changes would follow the changing structural pattern of international payments and would be used to adjust external imbalance. Instead, the IMF and most of its leading member governments chose to view the system as one of fixed rates, a new gold exchange standard in which an exchange standard was regarded as a symbol of stability and the new mercantilism was to defend that rate to the last. The opposing view, that the exchange rate is a price and is therefore subject to change; that it is, in fact, of all prices, the one whose changes are most effective in that they alter the relative price structure of countries – this was a view of which the implications were largely ignored. Variation of such a strategic price, used as a key control in economic policy, is too important to set aside.

Finally, there is in the record, as we have already argued, overwhelming evidence that speculation played a unique and destabilising role in the adjustable-peg system. Moreover, speculation grew greater and more perverse during the period the system obtained. The growth of a world capital market with huge off-shore balances seeking optimum security and tempting to use for exchange arbitrage, and the growth of international corporations operating and administering cash flows in many currencies were, in the 1950s and 1960s, features relatively new to the international monetary scene. They continue as major influences, but we now realise that they enormously complicate and intensify the disturbing forces to which the adjustable-peg system is subject.

(iii) Free rates – or nearly so

In economics, as in life, nothing quite turns out as it is expected to do. For twenty years, free rates of exchange had been advocated on the grounds that they were preferable to the adjustable-peg system.[1] Between 1970 and 1973, a world in which the leading currencies were allowed to have exchange rates which might be described as 'flexible', was established. Now we look back on a dozen years over which flexible rates have been the norm.

First, how has the system (if we can call it a system) worked? Institutionally the pattern which emerged in the mid-1970s was vestigial of many of the features of Bretton Woods. Multilateralism was still unimpaired, the co-operative spirit was still alive, expressed by the continuance of the Fund and the activities of

[1]It is difficult to say with whom the flood of advocacy began. Here are some of the writers: Milton Fiedman, 'The Case for Flexible Exchange Rates', *Essays in Positive Economics* (Chicago: University of Chicago Press, 1953) pp. 157–203; W. M. Scammell, 'What Sort of Exchange Rates?', *Westminster Bank Review*, May 1954; James Meade, 'The Case for Variable Exchange Rates', *Three Banks Review*, September 1955. In his book, *International Payments, Debts and Gold* (New York, Scribner's, 1964) pp. 356–9, Fritz Machlup gives an interesting list of the economists who advocated free exchange rates. The most notable book at a high level of discussion was Egon Sohmen's *Flexible Exchange Rates, Theory and Controversy* (Chicago, University of Chicago Press, rev. edn, 1969).

many international committees and working groups. A key-currency approach was increasingly stressed. Two aspects of the old system were, however, radically changed: the role of gold, and the function of exchange rates as a medium of balance-of-payments adjustment. In the original conception of Bretton Woods, gold had been an international numeraire in terms of which, through the gold-convertible dollar, all other currencies were expressed and their exchange rates fixed. After 1971 when the dollar was no longer convertible, all that was changed. Steps taken since the mid-1970s have sought progressively to demonetise gold, as a unit of account, a reserve asset and an intervention medium.

The new role of exchange rates was a piecemeal effort to provide a working system of balance-of-payments adjustment. The unsatisfactory performance of the adjustable-peg system, the growth over twenty years of academic support for free exchange rates, and the conviction by those who controlled matters that, in the racing tides of the 1970s, no fixed exchange rate could be held for long, all served to establish flexible exchanges for a long period of time.

Thus, if we return to fundamentals, that any international monetary system must have at least three characteristics – international money, an adjustment system, and control at the centre – then the first two of these had been radically altered from 1971 and the third had to fall into line to allow any sort of system to continue. International money was now reduced to two categories: key currencies held for reserves and for intervention, and SDRs available in limited amounts to members of the IMF. The adjustment system was supposed to be flexible exchange rates, and the IMF was forced to adapt itself to remain in the position of 'control' at the centre.

It is with the exchange-rate system that we are here concerned, so it is necessary to examine it more closely. In the first place, exchange rates were not free to fluctuate in response to supply and demand in the market save in varying degrees of surveillance by participant governments. Typically a given currency would be maintained by the intervention of its central bank at a value deemed by that country to be appropriate to its balance-of-payments position, conducive to maintaining a satisfactory level of reserves and, in most cases, in fixed relation to some key currency.

Table 5.1   Exchange rate arrangements for IMF currencies at 31 March 1986

	No. of countries	
Currency pegged to:		
US dollar	31	
French franc	14	
Other currency	5	
SDR	12	
Other currency composites	32	94
Exchange rate adjusted according to a set of indicators		5
Co-operative exchange arrangements		8
Other		41
		148

SOURCE: IMF, *International Financial Statistics* (monthly) (IMF, Washington).

Thus in March 1986 we had an exchange-rate pattern as shown in Table 5.1. At any given time a currency might be stable in relation to a chosen key currency, or depreciating or appreciating slowly in response to movements in the key currencies. In general one may say that it was common practice to seek a stable exchange rate in the short run but to allow long-run forces, as they became cumulatively strong, to manifest themselves. Thus for most leading currencies periods of exchange-rate change would be punctuated by periods of stability.

Perhaps the most striking thing about the present pattern of exchange rates is its resemblance not to the adjustable peg as it was but to the adjustable peg as it was intended to be. In the short run, fluctuations in the balance of payments affected the reserves; in the long run, such fluctuations would be adjusted by changes in the exchange rate. Moreover, since the rate changes were cumulative market changes and not discrete changes in a fixed rate, the chances of the rate being stabilised at an equilibrium level were enhanced. It might also have been argued in support of the new system that greater flexibility of rates would present speculators with a less attractive exchange market. Once-over rate changes of the adjustable-peg type can be guessed and profited from; continuous movements, since they do not reveal their trend until later, provide a more hazardous environment in which to operate. If we consider these attributes of the new system and couple them with the observable fact that, after 1974, the world demand for international liquidity so declined as to ease a problem which had been continuous since the war, we might be tempted to hail the new exchange-rate system as a success and counsel its indefinite retention. Such is, however, not the case. The present system is variously described in terms that are mostly pejorative. There is increasing unease with the way in which 'managed floating' works in practice, and even some nostalgia for the fixed-rate systems of the past. Where then has the new system failed?

The first reaction to such a question is, of course, that the international stresses of the 1970s and 1980s have been enormously greater than any forces to which the adjustable peg was subject in the 1946–71 period. The convulsions of that epoch were in the first ten post-war years, when Bretton Woods and the adjustable-peg system was cushioned by exchange controls, the Marshall Plan and the inconvertibility of currencies. Between 1955 and 1965 the economic climate was comparatively mild and equable. Industrial countries were growing at more or less comparable speeds, inflation rates were low and similar from country to country, primary-commodity prices were low for the importing countries, changes in the terms of trade were small. In spite of all this, the adjustable peg was under continual attack for its performance. Its weak performance was not the prime cause of the breakdown in the Bretton Woods system in 1971, but it is safe to say that the par-value system would, in any event, not have been sustainable in the 1970s which was to produce a world-energy crisis, a primary-commodity price inflation, widespread inflation of greater magnitude and incidence than ever before, and two international recessions, the second of which was the greatest break in economic growth since the 1930s. Assuming, however, that international monetary systems must be expected to survive some rough economic weather, what were the forces which would have made fixed exchange rates impossible in the 1970s and early 1980s?

The first force was that of changed economic circumstances. The forces required for balance-of-payments adjustment in the 1950s and 1960s were those which operated dominantly on the current account, and, by changing trade flows in response to relative prices of traded goods, would impel the exchange rate to hover closely around a purchasing-power parity value. As long as relative growth and inflation rates of countries were similar, the adjustable-peg system was capable of operating with only frictional difficulties. In the 1970s this condition was not fulfilled. Prices rose violently, incomes grew at disparate rates. Crises forced central banks into corrective policies of varying conflict with the circumstances. The stabilisers which had smoothed the ship's motion in a moderate sea were useless in the gales which now were prevalent.

Second, the long-standing assumption that adjustment of the balance of payments is made through the current account and that capital account movements are subsidiary and unimportant, was no longer tenable. With the growth of the capital market from a few national centres to a world market in which extra-territorial dealing in many currencies had to be added to the dealings in national centres, where flows of private-sector funds became of such a volume as to dwarf public-sector operations, the total of capital transactions in the balance of payments often became large enough to dwarf the visible and invisible transactions of the current account and their influence upon the exchange rate. From here onwards initiating forces and correcting forces had to be seen as operating on capital-account transfers. It is sufficient at this stage only to mention the forces which made such capital flows possible. Clearly, instant communication was a precondition. Growth of international banking was part cause and part result. The ramification of near-bank institutions to manage capital and distribute portfolios was an influence. So, too, was the proliferation of multinational corporations with international cash flows and working balances in many currencies. Then there were the central banks, which now held reserves in not one but a number of currencies and which were constantly switching and redistributing their holdings. On any given day in the foreign-exchange market the number of transactions which represented goods and services trading was a small proportion of the whole. Moreover, it became obvious as the 1970s passed that a new factor had entered into the field so far as speculation against currencies was concerned: no single central bank nor small group of central banks, could now, by intervention in the foreign-exchange market, defend a currency and prevent its depreciation (or appreciation). The speculative selling (or buying) pressure was now too large for official offsetting.

The third force which would have caused the adjustable peg to fail in the 1970s was the changed position of the US dollar as a reserve currency. As long as that currency could only be acquired by the non-dollar world through deficits in the US balance of payments, a check against the amount of dollar reserves existed. As soon, however, as it became possible to create extra-territorial dollars in the Euro-dollar market, the leverage of this control was reduced and dollars were available to deficit countries at large to service their deficits.

It is evident, then, that the changes in the international payments system in the 1970s were qualitative and called for new devices and a new approach to the basic economic problems, in particular to adjustment and the exchange rate. The problem now was (a) how to order exchange rates in a world in which capital movements and not relative prices of traded goods were the prime determinants of exchange rates, and (b) how to influence exchange rates in a market where central banks, acting singly or even in groups, did not possess the reserve resources to intervene effectively.

This problem was, and is, a formidable one. Central banks, using the only policy weapons they knew, attempted to control exchange rates, but capital movements, driven by the market expectations of many profit-seeking participants proved too much for effective intervention. Rates 'overshot' the purchasing-power parity levels which central bankers still saw as equilibrium target levels. The result was that official intervention became sporadic, and rates, influenced by capital movements, often went to levels which were, in terms of the trade items, untenable. It is, moreover, arguable that the intermittent but heavy intervention by central banks and the widespread swap arrangements to which they resorted merely made the market more unpredictable than otherwise and encouraged precautionary and speculative movements in and out of currencies. Thus the free-market exchange-rate system so long advocated by economists operated differently from the way expected[1] and to some extent went out of control. Too often in economics the problems of the long run have to be set

---

[1] One feature which was feared and made much of by opponents of floating exchange rates did not materialise, namely that the uncertainty of floating rates would constrain the growth of real trade.

aside, because events in the system demand inordinate short-run solutions. It was so with floating exchange rates. No sooner had floating become general in 1973 than a primary-commodity price inflation and OPEC's dramatic increase in the world oil price created unprecedented problems for the international economy. These were followed by a world recession in 1975, a quasi-recovery and a second oil-price crisis in 1979. Finally a world recession began in 1979 which lasted at least until 1983, the recovery from which has been fitful. These events encouraged improvisation and *ad hoc* policy interventions in which the floating-exchange-rate system had to be taken as given. It worked badly, but at least it did work. The best that can be said is that a decade of floating rates, operating under extreme conditions, has enabled us to see the system's defects. We have a diagnosis. Can we pass beyond this?

Let us go back to basics. The first requirement of a viable system is a form of international money. Since 1973 this requirement has been met by central banks' reserve holdings in the form of several currencies which are used for short-term exchange-market in-tervention. These are backed up by gold and IMF assets, both of which serve as reserves but require switching into currencies if they are to be used for intervention. Before 1971 the reserve currencies item consisted mainly of US dollars, the dollar holding the central position in the gold–dollar standard of Bretton Woods. What we now have is a multiple reserve currency situation.

A useful step forward would now be to make use of the concept of 'target zones' for exchange rates, which was advocated by the IMF in 1974,[1] and to consolidate the international reserve cur-rency supply by selecting a number of currencies to serve as reserves and to set the exchange rate between them. Thus we might conceive of the US dollar, the DM, the yen, the French franc and the British pound as constituting between them a zone of stable exchange rates. So long as this zone included the most significant trading nations then peripheral countries could stabilise their currencies relative to the zone countries.

The question arises as to which countries should compose the zone. Two criteria (other than their own acceptance) should

[1]*Guidelines for the Management of Floating Exchange Rates* (Washington, DC, IMF) pp. 21–30.

govern this: namely, size, and potential stability – that is, potential ability to maintain the zone. The minimum zone would be the United States, Germany and Japan. The addition of France and Britain would be a luxury but might produce difficulties, since Britain has been anxious to divest herself of the key-currency role and has hitherto refused to join the European Monetary Scheme. France might be an undesirable choice since she has repeatedly played the role of maverick in financial affairs and is prone to exploit situations for her own advantage. A final and perhaps best alternative would be to constitute the zone as the USA, Japan and EEC. Thus the dollar and the yen would be linked to the ECU to which, in turn, the major European currencies are linked.

A second basic of international monetary stability, namely the provision of an international adjustment system, would be served by the conditions under which a 'target zone' of exchange rates would have to operate. In order to stabilise exchange rates between members of the target zone the macro policies of the participants would have to be coordinated so that, as far as possible, exchange rates between them would stabilise. Thus the country group, or target zone, would play, in harness, the central role that was played by the USA under Bretton Woods or of Britain under the nineteenth-century gold standard. In the ideal model, the target zone could be enlarged by enlisting additional countries prepared to conform to its objectives and methods of working. In the most realistic model, a member country could fall out of the zone for the time being if it could not conform to zone rules.

The difficulties of implementing such a target-zone scheme as this would be enormous. Not least among the difficulties would be the task of coercing countries into membership. Germany has consistently turned away from any suggestion that the DM is a key currency. The United States is an essential starter but would be prone to use its weight within the group. Japan is an unknown quantity in international monetary affairs; not much has yet been asked of her but it would be unreal to take her compliance for granted.

This brings us to our final stability condition for the international monetary system – control at the centre. Assuming that order in exchange rates can be spread outwards from the nucleus of the target zone, who is to play the co-ordinating role? Clearly, to rely on one country, to say that in the triumvirate of EEC, USA and Japan any one entity will dominate, is unrealistic. The decisions to be taken as to prices, income, money supply, macro-control policies in general, are all such as to override national sovereignty. Rights of control of interest rates within the group, for example, are unlikely to be conceded by any single country to the others. This raises the inevitable question of whether the IMF can fulfil a central role. It is the logical next choice. But the record of the IMF, the power within it of the United States, the proneness to tie up decisions by 85 per cent majorities, and the making of major decisions in the whispering gallery of Washington, all make one doubt whether the Fund could be used for this purpose. Perhaps a small streamlined body consisting of the finance ministers of the target countries and their central bankers and equipped with a small élite secretariat would better fill the role. It would be wise for the target countries initially to co-ordinate only the direction of movement of their currencies. There is historical precedent for this and it could constitute a preliminary feeling of the way towards a tighter co-ordination of policies. Later an attempt might be made to confine exchange rates between the target countries within a band of allowable fluctuation. Ultimately and as experience grew this band could be adjusted.

It is easy from past experience to anticipate some of the issues which would divide the target countries. The most probable would be that within the group there would be deficit and surplus countries. In such a situation the question of who was to adjust the deficit would loom large. Should the deficit country deflate or the surplus country inflate? The Bonn Summit meeting in July 1978 demonstrated such a disagreement. The difficulties within the European Snake arrangement and the long history of the German surplus within the OEEC in the 1960s and 1970s demonstrate the difficulties of such a situation. The task of stabilising exchange rates is only a whisker away from that of having a world currency. If, between a group of countries, exchange rates remain absolutely stable then a common currency is within their grasp. We have for more than a dozen years observed the failure of EMS to achieve this goal.

To achieve exchange-rate stability it is necessary to achieve a common pattern of macro-policies. This presents the most difficult requirements in international economic policy – both in the economic and political fields. The alternative, however, is to suffer the disorder of freedom and unilateral action. Somewhere between total fredom of exchange rates, which implies disorder, and fixed exchange rates, which requires iron discipline and unanimity of purpose beyond our hopes, there must be some compromise condition. The target-zone approach, by stabilising the most important exchange rates and giving a nucleus of order which may spread wider as its advantages are realised, would give us a compromise that might be feasible.

6

Theoretical Approaches to Adjustment

(i) Introduction

Theories relating to adjustment of the balance of payments are deep-rooted in economic literature. They go back at least to the pre-Adam Smith writings of the mercantilists. But they have this in common: they are concerned with the maintenance of the balance of payments in relation to some stated norm. For the mercantilists, the desired norm consisted of an excess of exports over imports. The choice of this norm was justified politically by the contribution it made to the enrichment of the nation state. For the English economists of the nineteenth century, the norm was defined in terms of an equilibrium of foreign transactions such that it conformed to a general equilibrium system, variations in which were expressed by intra-country movements of some generally accepted monetary medium – in practical terms, gold. Thus the great difference between the views of adjustment before and after Adam Smith was that the earlier view valued accumulation of international money by country A at the expense of countries B, C and D, whereas the later view conceived of an equilibrium distribution of international money as between countries in the world system proportionate to the share of each in world output of goods and services.

In the 1940s came the Keynesian revolution, which had its own peculiar effects on international economic policy – some immediate, some delayed and taking the form of reactions to Keynesianism rather than Keynesianism itself. The immediate effects were, of course, the application of Keynesian macro economics to the open economy and the light that it shed upon the transmission and adjustment processes; the view of adjustment and exchange rates implicit in the Bretton Woods arrangements; the highlighting of the connection in a multi-country system between exchange rates and national rates of inflation and growth; and the interdependence of exchange-rate patterns and national macro-policies. The delayed or reactionary effects of Keynesianism came upon us in the 1960s and were the result of fundamental features in Keynesianism itself. Were we to array such fundamentals we would probably settle on the following: the possibility of equilibrium of national income at all sorts of levels, of which that peculiar to full utilisation of productive resources, particularly labour, is but one; the probable failure, save in unique and improbable circumstances, of any economy to generate sufficient monetary demand to take up its total output at full employment; the relation between saving and national capital formation and the role played in that relation by the rate of interest. These are all aspects of the Keynesian revolution which have been debated tirelessly by economists for over forty years. But the feature which encompasses all others, which is most fundamental and which has spilled its influence beyond economics into politics and to groups and governments indifferent to economic theorising, is this: there is no set of forces inherent in the capitalist system which leads an economy to an optimal set of conditions – price stability, full employment, equilibrium of the balance of payments; these can only be achieved by conscious intervention in the forces which shape the economy. With the establishment of this, bastions fell that were thereto considered inviolable. Adam Smith's invisible hand was denied its dexterity; Say's law was declared null and void; the beautiful simplicity of the market, the eternal tendency to adjust at an admirable equilibrium, was denied. The interference in economic processes of the state in order to achieve desirable aims was justified. The road to what was later to be called 'big government' was clearly indicated.

We are concerned in this chapter with the implications for the international economy of the economic doctrine of monetarism which was probably the strongest of the reactions to Keynes. Political hostility to Keynesianism need rest only on blind prejudice. Economists must have a foundation of scientific veracity. Politicians of the right, wishing to give their prejudices some aura of intellectual respectability, turned to monetarism as an economic *credo*. In itself the doctrine was not new. As a doctrine it is rooted in classical economics; as a series of policy prescriptions it emerged in the 1950s and 1960s in the writings of certain American and Canadian economists;[1] but until the end of the post-war high-growth period in the early 1970s it did not emerge from academic seclusion, nor did it develop distinct prescriptions on the main international variables such as the exchange rate and the balance of payments.

In this chapter we shall divide our attention among three matters: first, a discussion of monetarism as a general economic doctrine; second, a brief account of its specific bearing on the problems of the international monetary system; and third, a brief look at the significance of both for international monetary policy.

(ii) Monetarism

Monetarism is not a coherent system of thought which may be presented as a set of models. Rather it is a culling from the economic thought of the last two centuries of such strands as may serve to knit together a patchwork of ideas. Moreover, since this culling has been done by many writers in a scattered literature of books, articles and professional papers and seldom brought together in a single exposition, it presents a challenge if it is to be fairly presented.[2] The best means is to set forth the doctrine as a number of theoretical propositions and policy prescriptions whilst realising that even these may be differently emphasised according to person and period. Such a set of propositions might involve the following:

(1) Monetarist analysis of the economy in terms of a quantity theory of money is derived generally from classical theory. More immediately, monetarism as policy prescription is

[1] I am thinking here of Milton Friedman, Harry Johnson and Robert Mundell.

[2] For a good, though biased, discussion of monetarism, see D. Laidler, 'Monetarism: An Interpretation and an Assessment', *Economic Journal*, March 1981, pp. 1–29.

rooted in the Friedman assertion that growth of the money supply should be controlled, and that in an expanding economy such control should hold monetary growth to a rate *pari passu* with the growth of domestic product.

(2) Strong scepticism of the Phillips curve trade-off between inflation and unemployment. Monetarists assert the existence of 'inherent stability' of the private sector if emancipated from monetary disturbances.

(3) An assertion that balance-of-payments deficits and surpluses are essentially monetary phenomena.

(4) Attempts to 'stabilise' the economy either by fiscal or monetary policies are foredoomed to failure largely because they are inevitably based on past data. This, and difficulties of controlling fiscal and monetary policy tools, explains why disturbances to the economy emanate so often from the financial sector. In contrast, the real sector of the economy is inherently stable.

(5) There exists in the economy a natural rate of unemployment, which is determined by structural characteristics of the economy, the preference scale of workers as between work and leisure, rates of technical change, changes in the composition and size of the labour force, the degree of unionisation, and many other factors. It is only through changes in these structural characteristics that the natural rate of unemployment can be altered. It cannot be manipulated by changes in aggregate demand.

It is not possible or desirable here to launch into *seriatim* discussion of this set of precepts. It is, however, possible to see from them how monetarism, as they define it, can result either from hostility to Keynesianism and its implications for government intervention, or from a dislike of government intervention as such and a search for an economic philosophy which precludes it. It is not difficult to see from these precepts how monetarism makes its appeal to the political 'right', and how it has ridden the crest of the wave of conservatism that has swept the West in the 1970s and 1980s. Monetarism essentially amounts to a claim, of varying insistence, that the economic system is best left to itself. Thus it is stable: markets tend to desirable equilibria; relations such as the demand for money function are obligingly stable. The system does not so much need management as it needs a governor, in the sense of a constant-speed flywheel. This is provided by consistency in the quantity of money. It is interference with the mechanisms which leads to breakdown and malfunction.

Against this general background the monetarist view of the international monetary system falls into place. The balance of payments is essentially a monetary phenomenon, in as much as the deficit or surplus which is its key feature is reflected in the variances of the 'monetary movements' section of the account. It is this monetary variable which is of significance, since for the rest the balance of payments always balances by the processes of double-entry bookkeeping. This is not, of course, to deny that balance-of-payments surpluses or deficits may be non-monetary as to causation. It simply affirms their location in the money account in response to whatever flows of funds have been induced by exogenous forces in the goods and securities flows of the current and capital accounts respectively. Given, then, that the monetary approach focuses on the excess or shortfall of money payments in and out of the economy as the strategic variable of the balance of payments, the domestic money supply and the domestic flow demand for money come into their own as forces which affect the balance of payments. A few examples illustrate this argument. If there is a deficit in the balance of payments, then payments to foreigners exceed payments by foreigners to the country concerned. There is a depletion of the domestic money supply and, with unchanged demand for cash balances, interest rates rise, attract short-term funds from abroad and adjust the balance of payments. For a surplus the processes work in the opposite directions.

None of this would have been denied by pre-monetarist economists. It is, after all, merely a simple account of what happened under the late-nineteenth-century gold standard. What is new is the emphasis. Where the existence of a deficit formerly prompted a search for explanation of the deficit in the goods flows, and advocated adjustment by alteration of relative prices within the goods markets, the monetarist approach drives its exponents to an examination of behavioural forces in the money market and, by inference, to consider the effects of interference by the central bank in the purely monetary variables.

The monetary approach to the balance of payments has a long history broken only by the interruption of the Keynesian revolution: that is, for practical purposes, from the early 1930s to the early 1960s, when economists were preoccupied with the relationship of the balance of payments to full employment. Prior to, say, 1931, the monetary approach derives from many writers: its view of world markets from Mill, and of the distribution among individual states of world money from Ricardo, Hume, Mill and Hawtrey. But these early derivations were eclectic and are only discernible now in the light of more modern emphases of monetarist ideas. It was not until well into the post Second World War period that the monetary approach to the balance of payments became a broad and discernible stream.

Two economists laid the foundations of the modern monetarist approach to the balance of payments: Harry Johnson and Robert Mundell. Johnson, in his fine article 'Towards a General Theory of the Balance of Payments',[1] moved adjustment theory forward from where Sydney Alexander had left it in a pseudo-Keynesian backwater, and gave it the distinctive monetarist characteristics. Johnson himself claims[2] that his work at this period was negatively derivative from James Meade's *magnum opus* of 1951, *The Theory of International Economic Policy, Vol. 1, The Balance of Payments*, a work of which he was highly critical, not only for its taxonomic approach but for the strongly Keynesian flavour of parts of its theory and policy prescriptions. However that may be, Johnson's subsequent work on balance-of-payments theory moved steadily away from Meade and from such writers as followed Meade's approach to the subject. He argued and established the balance of payments as a monetary phenomenon and its manipulation as being through monetary procedures. Devaluation, at that time a constant focus of attention, he singled out as the major expenditure-switching policy, and unlike his contemporaries, who analysed its effects in terms of the elasticities approach, he cast it in a monetary setting by relating it to the quantity of money.

Mundell, like Johnson, started from the premise that the balance of payments was a monetary variable best controllable by monetary policy. From this his thinking followed two important lines which he developed skilfully and with great effect on the later

[1] *International Trade and Economic Growth* (London, 1958) pp. 153–68.

[2] *The Monetary Approach to the Balance of Payments*, ed. H. G. Johnson and Jacob A. Frenkel (London, Allen & Unwin, 1976) p. 30.

development of monetarist thought on the balance of payments. Moreover, he expanded the focus of balance-of-payments analysis by including in his two developments the capital account of the balance of payments, which had hitherto been regarded as the residual section reflecting only the prime-moving influences at work in the current account. Starting from the assumption of free international capital mobility, Mundell went on to examine (i) the nature of the conflict between internal and external stability of an economy and how the tools of monetary and fiscal policy could be combined, with fixed exchange rates, to secure both the objectives of full employment and balance-of-payments equilibrium, and (ii) the significance for national control of the money supply of free entry and exit of capital. It is not possible to follow these lines of thought for any distance, but their significance for balance-of-payments theory can be glimpsed from even a cursory examination. In the case of fiscal and monetary policy and their use to secure internal and external equilibrium, the coupling of the mix was shown to be crucial. If fiscal policy were to be used to pursue external stability and monetary policy to pursue domestic stability, the result would be progressive divergence from the desired equilibrium of both. Starting from a position of initial deficit in the external balance this coupling of fiscal and monetary policies would have perverse effects on the interest rate. Domestic contraction of the economy (a conventional natural policy reaction to a deficit) by monetary policy would demand a rise in the interest rate. This would have the balance-of-payments effect of drawing funds from abroad into the capital account, while the budget surplus incurred by fiscal policy to meet the deficit would lower interest rates and induce capital to leave the capital account. This coupling of policies is therefore not feasible. If, however, fiscal policy be used to deal with internal equilibrium, and monetary policy to control the foreign balance, this policy mix is practicable and the results are beneficial. The effect on the interest rate from both fiscal and monetary policies in response to a deficit, is to raise the rate with beneficial effects on capital inflows to correct the deficit. Mundell showed that for this coupling there was a progressive convergence on domestic and external equilibrium.

This conclusion had great significance for the development of adjustment theory. Meade, from his book in 1951, had advocated two policy weapons to correct a deficit: the exchange rate for external control, and fiscal or monetary policy for control of domestic expenditure. Mundell was able to demonstrate that with a fixed exchange rate it was possible to control both external and internal stability with the two policy weapons of fiscal and monetary policy, if these were correctly deployed. Thus the exchange rate could be set aside as a policy tool or viewed in whatever other context might seem appropriate.

Mundell's second line of thought changed the view of the money supply. With recognition of the existence of capital mobility and the increasing scope, particularly after 1959, of the international capital market, he argued that the money supply of an open economy could not be exogenously set by the central bank. If this was the case then external monetary policy had to be reviewed. It seemed to have two facets: the first was to manipulate interest rates to influence capital flows as part of the fiscal/monetary policy coupling; the second was to influence international reserves and relieve the constraint which they might place on the other aspects of policy.

We have already said enough of the monetary approach to the balance of payments to differentiate it from the elasticities approach which it was intended to replace. This concentrated on the real aspects of the current account, examining how, by devaluation or direct controls on imports and exports, trade balances might be influenced. The monetary approach denied the validity or even the policy utility of this approach. Its basic tenet was that 'the balance-of-payments effects of any policy measure cannot be properly analysed without specifying the monetary consequence of the policy itself'.[1] By this tenet a tariff or a devaluation improves the balance of payments only if it induces an excess demand for money which generates changes through the credit system.

Since the exchange rate is the most important variable bearing upon the balance of payments we must be curious as to where it fits into the monetarist scheme of things. Here again, however, we have no formal system to refer to, no ironclad set of rules; we can only search out from the writings of the faithful such precepts as are relevant. Long before 1970, monetarists, not least Friedman,

[1]Most of Robert Mundell's salient contributions to international economics are contained in his *International Economics* (New York, 1968). His purely monetary viewpoint reaches its highest refinement in his *Monetary Theory* (Pacific Palisades, 1971).

argued that the diversity of national inflation rates implied flexibility of exchange rates, if only as a precondition of the pursuit of monetarist policies in individual countries.[1] The export of inflation by the USA in the later 1960s was in part blamed upon the fixed-rate regime of the IMF. Moreover, the monetarists have been the upholders of free markets and the role of the market in general economic equilibrium. More particularly, monetary markets must be free for perennial portfolio readjustment and monetary readjustment, and the foreign-exchange market is no exception. Under fixed exchange rates, balance-of-payments deficits result in changing international reserves for the countries concerned, who thereby are deprived of full monetary control of their economies; under flexible rates a deficit generates changes in exchange rates but not in reserves, thereby strengthening national monetary control. Yet the monetarists' views of exchange-rate behaviour are by no means uniform. For Harry Johnson and Mundell the approach was guarded. Johnson saw exchange-rate changes as expenditure-switching policies with a role to play in balance-of-payments adjustment; but that still leaves the question as to whether exchange-rate changes should be discrete, as under an adjustable-peg system, or continuous, as under a flexible regime. The question of fixed or free exchange rates is related to but separate from the one that asks whether the exchange rate is an effective medium of balance-of-payments adjustment. Some monetarists would deny the latter, some exhibit ambivalence as to the former. Mundell, whose theoretical views in the 1950s and 1960s were surprisingly consistent, held different views on the flexibility of exchange rates as he moved among his various sets of policy prescriptions. Other monetarists, arguing that no efficient monetary policy was possible under a fixed-rate regime, demanded flexible rates in the 1960s, but recoiled from what they observed in the free-rate regime of the 1970s and demanded 'some form of "orderly" conduct',[2] – whatever that may mean. Probably the best that we can say is that the monetarists incline towards support of

[1] *The Monetary Approach to the Balance of Payments*, ed. J. A. Frenkel and Harry G. Johnson, p. 42.

[2] It should be noted, however, that monetarists were not alone in advocacy of flexible exchange rates in the 1960s. James Meade, certainly no monetarist, led a vocal clamour by many Keynesian economists for an end of the adjustable-peg system.

flexible exchange rates providing such rates involve only minimal public intervention in the foreign-exchange market; that a devaluation has monetary effects, most notable of which is that it enables the money supply to be replenished after a deficit has reduced foreign-money holdings – that is, the reserves; and that whatever effects devaluation may have upon relative prices are secondary in their effects on the balance of payments to the important monetary effects.

(iii) Monetarism and policy

In the 1970s the monetarists have had the best of the running. Not only have the theorists established themselves upon the firm middle ground of macro economics, but they have – by their claims to economic legitimacy founded upon the 'respectable' writers of the past, by their propositions about the demand for money; their claimed relationships between money and money income; their analysis of money flows and inflation; and their ability to explain the breakdown of Bretton Woods and the adjustable peg system and the spread of inflation in the 1970s in terms of the impact of the US external deficit on the world economy under fixed exchange rates – by all this they have gained theoretical recognition and acceptability. It is indeed an impressive achievement, so much so that one prominent monetarist claims that 'we are all monetarists now.'[1] Maybe so, but there is still much to be said.

Given that there is at least widespread partial acceptance of monetarist theoretical precepts and that monetarists and non-monetarists blend and blur in what they believe and preach, it is in the field of economic policy that monetarism becomes distinct and differentiated. It has emerged as the successor of Keynesianism and as the determinant of public policy in the new right-wing governments of the West – in Britain under Thatcher, in the USA under Reagan, in West Germany under Kohl, in Canada under Mulroney, and elsewhere under such political flotsam as the current wave of anti-collectivism has thrown into power. Monetarist elements are now included in varying degree in the policies of

[1]Jacob Frenkel, in *The International Monetary System: Forty Years After Bretton Woods*, Conference held in May 1984, sponsored by the Reserve Bank of Boston, p. 120.

many Western countries, and the doctrine has revealed its weaknesses in its lack of uniformity.

Monetarism has always had its weakness in this lack of uniformity, which really arises from the vagueness with which the basic doctrine relates to policy. Unlike Keynesianism, which gave a convenient sense of simplicity in its manipulation of the macroeconomic aggregates, monetarism cannot be simply expressed as an economic doctrine with a recognised set of operational tools. The best minds among the monetarist economists gave their attention to theory, lesser men interpreted the theoretical implications for policy. Politicians took from the doctrine what suited them: the appeal to the mechanism of the market; the use of all sorts of monetary tools and devices; the tolerance to unemployment which would quell trade unionism and interference with the labour market; the claim that much unemployment was voluntary and could be mopped up by acceptance of a lower real wage. This difficulty in the interpretation of monetarism by its protagonists has created a policy confusion in the 1970s and 1980s which has been a salient feature of the period, resulting in tentative policies, obstinate experiments persevered in too long, and mistaken use of policy tools in half-understood situations. This confusion is worth some thought. It results from difficulties and wilful error in the practical application of monetarism. What have been the problems?

First has been the problem of where monetary policy starts. The Friedmanite prescription for price stability, of holding growth in the money supply at a rate *pari passu* with the growth of domestic product, was one intended for the maintenance of price stability in an already stable economy. It was, as Laidler says,[1] a prescription for staying out of trouble. In the 1970s, and by the time monetarism was appealed to by policy-makers, economies were already in trouble. The question was not how to preserve stability but how to retrieve it from an already unstable situation. On this question monetarists have been at variance with each other. Their solutions have varied from that of applying control of the money supply to a rate of modest growth and expecting after a time-lag that all would be well, to resorting to *ad hoc* measures to quell inflation after which orthodox monetarist methods could be

[1]Laidler, 'Monetarism', p. 18.

applied. Laidler admits a dilemma here. He admits there is much less unanimity among monetarists 'about how to tackle the problem of restoring stability than there is about how to maintain it'.[1] For him, achieving stability in the 1970s forced choices about what form of 'gradualism' should be used in order to get on track. In the various devices of which this gradualism has consisted, many weaknesses have been revealed, some of which are and some of which are not defects of monetarism.

The second policy problem of monetarism has been that of measurement. If money supply is to be controlled, how shall the money supply be defined? Is it desirable to control only the M1 of cash plus immediately usable bank deposits, or must the control be wider to embrace the whole field of credit channelled through the banking system? Several working definitions of the money supply have been tried but precision and success have been elusive. Only in Canada was there in the late 1970s any success in holding the money supply to a growth path. In Britain and the United States there was confusion. Failure to realise that manipulating the money supply affected interest rates and then refusing to accept the interest rates which resulted, brought the experiments to a point where they declined into mere guesswork. In Germany and Switzerland monetary control influenced the exchange rates in ways which the monetary authorities were not prepared to accept.

The third problem which has dogged monetarism in practice has been the large budget deficits with which it has had to coexist. To already large levels of government outlay have been added, as unemployment has grown, the burden of rising unemployment-benefit and welfare payments. From 1980 the Reagan-impelled outlays on 'defence' have swollen budget deficits to unprecedented levels. This in time has driven governments to excessive budget-balancing exercises. Public outlays have been ruthlessly trimmed at the fringes, while the politically inviolable centre-blocs of expenditure, defence and the social services, have remained intact. Monetarist economics has become associated with the expenditure-trimming exercises. It is unfortunate that monetarism, a respectable economic doctrine, should be politicised and associated with the unreason of Reaganite policies and with 'the squalor of Thatcherite Britain'.

---

[1]Laidler, 'Monetarism', p. 22.

Finally, there is the fatal flaw in monetarist gradualism: that it rested on the assertion that inflation could be broken only if disinflationary policies were tough enough and were persisted in long enough. Although inflation rates have declined, it has been at the cost of high unemployment rates, which still persist, and damage to the industrial sector, as firms and industries succumb to deflation. Monetarist apologetics for this process have not endeared it to electorates. Only the widespread political swing to the right has made such arguments acceptable. Once more it has politicised economics and economists, polarised policies, and led to a confusion in policy which, like the recession itself, has no precedent since the 1930s.

(iv) Monetarism and international policy

The argument of this chapter is that the monetary approach to the balance of payments has been a useful development in the academic literature of what we have come to call 'international adjustment'. It has concentrated attention on aspects of the adjustment process – money flows, interest rates, the monetary movements section of the balance-of-payments account – which were formerly regarded as incidental rather than central. As a result, we know more about how the balance of payments works; how it reacts to non-monetary forces.

It is on the prescriptive side that the monetary approach is weakest. This is partly because the prescriptions for policy are themselves tentative, and partly because the monetary institutions through which they must work are in many cases unsuitable, having grown piecemeal in response to varied stimuli. Moreover, the better monetarists have been theorists, and the doctrine has not developed a strong institutional wing to study and mould the forces through which it can best function. Unlike Keynesian economics which was created and aimed directly at the problem it was supposed to solve, namely involuntary unemployment, monetarism evolved slowly and theoretically, partly in reaction to Keynesianism and without any clear prescriptive policy capable of being applied in general circumstances. It was then in the 1970s adopted by the rising politicians of the right, and applied willy-nilly to the most puzzling and threatening economic conditions of the last half-century.

In the international sphere, monetarism has had fewer baneful effects than in the field of domestic macro policy, where its supposed applications and logical policies have been given free rein. There is no reason to argue that international monetary developments would have been very different in its absence. Indeed, such influence as it has had has been beneficial rather than otherwise. In a time when the capital account of the balance of payments has been seen to be important, monetarism has directed attention to international money flows and indirectly to international monetary institutions. Once we think in monetarist terms, excessive preoccupation with the trade balance is precluded. The salient problems of the international monetary system – international liquidity, exchange rates, the transmission and adjustment processes – are best approached by the monetarist route.

7

The Role and Mechanism of Capital Flows

(i) Introduction

Economists now over the age of fifty were brought up on the view that current-account transactions dominated the balance of payments. Capital-account balance was regarded as either subsidiary to, or invoked to change in, adjustment of the prime-moving balance of trade. That view has had to be modified. The national capital markets with which the pre-1939 world was dotted have been progressively (especially since the late 1950s) replaced by an international capital market, in which, by electronic and telecommunications media, transactions are concluded instantaneously across frontiers, oceans and continents; in which funds move ceaselessly in volumes never before dreamed of; and in which scrutiny of investment options and prospects are as swift and ubiquitous as the transactions. For some economies, capital movements dominate the balance of payments and may in themselves initiate the mechanics of the whole account.

The new-found importance of the capital account lies in the huge volume of transactions which are located there. This, in turn, has a twofold significance. First, movements of capital funds are now potentially so great that their effect on the exchange rate cannot be offset by exchange-fund operations in the opposite direction. The reserve holdings of any central bank, perhaps even of a group of central banks, may be insufficient to regulate the exchange rate in a direction contrary to market expectations. The second significant change of attitude that is necessary is that it must now be expected that balance-of-payments disequilibrium may be initiated by autonomous capital-account movement and the whole process of adjustment thought through in terms of capital-induced effects. In this chapter we shall first examine some of the implications of this change of view. In Section (iii) we shall look at some institutional capital-market changes which have created the new situation. In Section (iv) we shall look at the problem of external debt created by the large capital movements of the 1970s and early 1980s. All these matters bear heavily on our main theme of the stability of the international monetary system.

(ii) Capital flows in theory

The theory of capital flows is neither extensive nor satisfactory. Economic theorising is usually driven by events and by the necessity for general explanations, and the view that the current account was the driving force of the balance of payments led to theoretical concentration on the mechanics of that variable. After all, large capital flows were the result of rich countries with high savings rates seeking investment opportunities for high-risk investment. Such phenomena were observable *ex post*, and the empirical literature is replete with studies of British nineteenth-century overseas investment, Canadian capital imports in the last years of the nineteenth century, the real wealth transfer implicit in reparations payments, and so on. This writing highlighted the capital-transfer problem as it appeared in a period of rapid economic development. A good example is Jacob Viner's well-known study of Canadian borrowing between 1900 and 1913. In this, Viner showed how the inflow of funds to Canada from the London capital market and elsewhere, was through the price-specie-flow mechanism allowed to raise domestic prices in Canada and create an import surplus comparable in magnitude to the borrowing. But in the inter-war period, the problem of capital flows was raised in a context which required a more general theory. Given that defeated Germany was to honour her reparations obligations under the Versailles Treaty, how was the real transfer of wealth between Germany and her creditors to be effected? Keynes and Ohlin in a historic controversy laid the foundations of the theory of capital transfer.[1] The result of the controversy may be quickly summarised. Given that an international capital transfer, typically a loan, had to take place, how would the transfer be made in real terms? Two accounts of the process are required: first with a fixed exchange rate between the two countries, second with a free rate of exchange. Suppose that England made a loan to Canada. The money borrowed on the London capital market would be exchanged in the foreign-exchange market for Canadian dollars. Funds would flow out of England into Canada. English interest rates would be raised, and this combined with the diminution in the English money supply would lower prices in England. Meanwhile, in Canada, prices would be raised as funds flowed in and interest rates fell. The change in relative price levels would induce a current-account surplus in England and deficit in Canada. The change in the balance of trade would effect the real transfer. The real transfer of goods then reverses the process. England's export surplus causes funds to flow to London, the Canadian import surplus causes funds to flow out of Canada. When the total capital of the loan in real terms has been transferred the money movement has been completely reversed.

This classical view of the transfer process made several simplifying assumptions. It assumed, for example, that the marginal propensity of the borrowing country to import and the marginal propensity of the borrower to spend the loan proceeds abroad, were the same. There is no reason why they should be. Apart from this, the whole reasoning relied on acceptance of the quantity theory of money and its concomitant assumption of full employment. Also it made the usual classical assumption of high elasticities of demand for imports and exports in both countries.

When we relax the assumption of fixed exchange rates the model is little changed. The export of money from England to Canada depreciates the pound and appreciates the dollar. This generates an English export surplus and Canadian import surplus as before. When all the loan proceeds are transferred and the real transfer through the export surplus is completed, the sterling exchange rate appreciates to its former level.

---

[1] J. M. Keynes, 'The German Transfer Problem', and Bertil Ohlin, 'The Reparation Problem: A Discussion', *Economic Journal*, 1929.

It is evident that the transfer process by creating an export surplus in the capital-exporting country is, in essence, the same process as is employed for adjusting a balance-of-payments disequilibrium. This is not surprising since, in essence, a capital transfer is but a special case of balance-of-payments disequilibrium. The capital transfer is a 'unilateral' payment within the balance of payments; it involves an outflow of money only from the home country. If international transactions are initially in balance the capital movement produces disequilibrium in independently motivated transactions.

The controversy between Keynes and Ohlin had centred around the *modus operandi* of this classical transfer model. Keynes had argued that Germany's reparations transfer could not be made because Germany could not achieve the necessary export surplus. The demand for her exports was too inelastic for her to achieve it by lowering prices. Ohlin was not impressed by an elasticities approach. A quarter-century ahead of time he wanted to consider the transfer problem in terms of income and not price differentials. There was a surprising reversal of roles in this famous controversy: Keynes, the later founder of modern income theory, talking in classical terms of price-driven changes in the terms of trade; Ohlin talking of income and sensing the existence of wider forces than those of price.

When we turn to the modern theory of capital transfer we take account of income changes as primary forces. As in the income theory of balance-of-payment adjustment, income forces are not sufficient, save under unrealistic assumptions, to complete the adjustment. In this case the income effects are, in themselves, sufficient to bring about the real transfer of the loan, only under assumptions which preclude reality – for example, that the marginal propensity to save in the borrowing country is zero, or that there is sufficient compensation from induced investment to boost income to that point where all the leakages other than saving are equal to the original injection.[1] The income model of capital transfer shows that, for the whole of the real transfer to be effected, other forces, including price changes, must enter the

---

[1] The model is worked through in detail in my *International Trade and Payments* (London, Macmillan 1974) pp. 374–9.

picture. From the smoothness and swiftness with which all but the largest adjustments appear to be made in practice the aggregate force of these other influences must be great.

The exchange rate, if it is free, may also play a part in real capital transfer, supplementing the effects of interest-rate changes. As funds leave the lending country its exchange rate depreciates. This cheapens its exports and raises, relative to home goods, the price of its imports. Not only is the necessary export surplus created in the lending country but the income changes necessary to create the trade balance are supplemented by the exchange rate. In the recipient country the currency is bid up by the transfer of funds, the appreciation helping the income effects to create the necessary trade deficit.

We may sum up this cursory sketch of capital-transfer theory by the following:

(1) In the capital-exporting country there must be a trade surplus, and in the capital-importing country a trade deficit.
(2) These foreign-balance changes will be brought about by income fall in the capital-exporting country and income rise in the capital-importing country.
(3) There will occur also a change in the net barter terms of trade between the two countries, in favour of the transferee and against the transferor.
(4) The transfer problem may be viewed in two ways: (i) as a special case of the theory of adjustment, where large unilateral payments within the capital section of the balance of payments must have their compensating adjustment in the current account; or (ii) as a series of special problems manifesting themselves in a particular context, each with its own peculiar circumstances, background and political trappings – as a reparatious transfer facing an impoverished Germany in the 1920s, as the capital imports of Canada over several decades of her development, or as the United States in 1983–5 with an insatiable need for funds to finance a budget deficit generated by defence outlays. To this last case we will now pay some attention.

Capital movements dominate the American balance of payments. Empirical evidence shows that during an expansion in the

United States relative to the rest of the world, the American balance of payments strengthens as a result of funds moving to the USA. In conditions of floating exchange rates the dollar appreciates. In the years since the Second World War this process has been repeated in 1960–1, 1963–5, 1975–7, and 1982–5. We shall examine the last phase.

In 1982, the United States, under the influence of fiscal policy generated largely by burgeoning defence expenditures, began to pull out of the severe recession which had begun in 1979. By 1983 the unemployment rate had fallen four percentage points, the inflation rate had dropped significantly and real growth had increased – stagflation in reverse. Moreover, the United States was the leader out of recession. In Canada, the UK, Germany, France and Japan similar trends were discernible but to a much smaller extent. Accompanying this expansion in the United States was a great increase in the deficit on current account. For 1981–3 the trade balance on goods, services and private transfers was +$10.7 billion, –$3.8 billion and –$35.5 billion.[1] Of the six other leading industrial countries,[2] two had large increases in their surpluses, one had a deterioration of a longstanding deficit, one had a moderate fall in a long-standing surplus and the others showed only minor change. Clearly the US trading position had altered drastically during the expansion. In a condition of floating exchange rate and minimal intervention by the US authorities in the foreign-exchange market, the current-account deficit was matched by a large increase in net capital import in the capital account, coupled with a steady rise in the dollar exchange rate starting in early 1981. At the time of writing (early 1986), the dollar remains a very strong currency.

The increasing deficit in the US current account can be attributed to various causes; notable among them a large worsening of the non-oil trade deficit, reduced by a very moderate positive swing in the oil balance. Wallich estimates that in 1984 the non-oil trade deficit increased by $100 billion, of which one-quarter was assignable to the expansion of the US economy relative to the rest of the world, about 15 per cent to the difficulties of debt-burdened developing countries (for example, Mexico, Brazil), and the

---

[1] IMF *Annual Report*, 1984, Washington, p. 23.
[2] Canada, Japan, France, Germany, Italy and the UK.

remainder, at least 50 per cent, to the rise in the value of the US dollar and its effect on American exports.[1] Two forces have offset the deficit: the rise in capital imports, and the appreciation of the exchange rate. It is impossible to distribute the correction accurately between the two forces. All we can do is to guess that even without the dollar rise there would have been a large current-account deficit which would have been corrected in the capital account with no effect on the exchange rate. To the extent that there has been appreciation of the rate (and it has been considerable) there has been over-correction which in turn has had its influence on the current account. Apart from these fairly mechanistic imprecisions there is the fact that in 1982 the USA was leading the way out of the deepest and most prolonged recession since the 1930s, and that a very large volume of private-sector liquidity in the world capital market was seeking a secure and profitable national venue of investment. The large American deficit and the defence-programme outlays which impended promised high interest rates. Security and high yield could scarcely fail to draw funds. They did, and when the import of capital itself prevented interest rates from rising[2] the expansion was sustained by rising real investment. At the time of writing the process is still incomplete. Excess demand for dollars remains high, and a high current-account deficit is its concomitant. If the excess-demand function for dollars were to disappear the dollar exchange rate would have to depreciate to such an extent as to eliminate the deficit on current account.

While remaining within the legitimate bounds of capital-transfer theory we can accommodate both cases that have occurred historically:[3] the nineteenth-century case of the mature country which for a variety of reasons achieved a long-run surplus on current-account and then exported capital; and the capital-importing country which adjusted the balance of payments by a current-account deficit. In the former case the current account initiated the process, in the latter case the balance-of-payments structure was primarily determined by the capital account.

[1]H. Wallich, 'Capital Movements – the Tail that Wags the Dog' in *The International Monetary System* (Federal Reserve Bank of Boston, 1984) p. 180.

[2]They fell from the beginning of 1982.

[3]Omitting the reparations case.

Interested as we are in this book in the stability of the international monetary system, what reactions may we have to the US dollar exchange rate and current trade account being determined by the level of capital imports? The first reaction is that the present situation, which from the US viewpoint at any rate looks stable enough, is, on historical precedent, characteristic only of the expansion phase of the cycle. We may then expect the situation to unwind itself when the upswing has run its course. A probable scenario would be as follows. A darkening of economic horizons with dipping economic indicators of growth and employment would check confidence in the dollar, causing withdrawals of funds and bringing about a reduction in the exchange rate. This might quicken in speed and volume, causing progressive depreciation, which in its turn would reduce the current-account deficit, turning it, if the capital export were prolonged and depreciation continued, into a surplus.

A second reaction to the dynamic character of the US capital account is that it is characteristic of the role of the US dollar as a reserve currency. As long as the currency is in other respects acceptable in this role, the world will use it as such, and the USA is duty-bound not to modify the role by any form of exchange control. Indeed, even if the US government were minded to do so, it is not capable of making such control effective. Movements of the dollar in off-shore markets are controlled and influenced by countries other than the USA, and if the US government wishes to avoid sudden withdrawals of foreign funds it should pursue policies calculated to hold foreign funds in the USA, particularly to seek low inflation rates and high real interest rates. It is possible to envisage conditions where, expansionary monetary policies and rising inflation rates giving rise to panic foreign withdrawals of funds, this could, particularly with the large fiscal deficit of the USA, create a cycle of inflation and exchange-rate depreciation ending one knows not where.

The conclusion appears to be that the capital-importing (and largely capital-determined) US economy is like a fast car. Wisely and carefully driven, speed itself imposes little risk, but inattention, ill-judgement or a moment of panic can bring disaster. There is no other major industrial country at present which can indulge simultaneously in fiscal expansion, capital inflows and a high exchange rate. The price for this unique advantage should be probity, care and precision on the part of the US monetary authorities.

(iii) The Euro-currency market

To any consideration of capital-flow problems in the modern international system the Euro-currency market is central. It has become since its inception in the early 1950s the entrepôt centre for the capital movements of the world. 'It has created a truly international money market, and has developed a structure of international interest rates that is entirely without precedent.'[1] We must pause to examine its functions.

The market arose after 1958 when convertibility of Western European currencies was restored and London, in the new-found absence of exchange control, was able to resume its place as a leading financial market for international funds. Prior to 1958 'traditional foreign-exchange banking' prevailed.[2] Banks in Holland accepted deposits, either from foreigners or domestic nationals, only in guilders, and made guilder loans. Canadian banks accepted only Canadian dollars on deposit. Foreign trade was financed by national banks obtaining foreign currencies, spot or forward, in the international interbank market, or drawing on foreign-currency balances held in correspondent banks abroad. This system had developed as trade had developed in the nineteenth century, and followed naturally from the assumption that a nation's banks administered the nation's money. It was quite sufficient for international trade and payments that this system only should exist. Much of the great expansion of trade in the 1950s and 1960s took place on this basis. The inference in most discussions of international payments still is that this is the only system. Beside it, however, has grown the Euro-currency system,

[1]Paul Einzig, *The Euro-Dollar System*, 5th edn (London, Macmillan, 1973) p. 4.

[2]Ronald I. McKinnon, *Money in International Exchange* (Oxford University Press, 1979) p. 198. McKinnon uses the initials TFEB as an acronym for the simple system of on-shore banking in which foreign-exchange business was conducted between domestic banks and correspondent banks abroad.

which has a profound effect on the current and capital transactions in foreign currencies.

Clearly the Euro-currency market, which has grown swiftly and almost spontaneously since 1958 with no official support from governments, must meet some deep-felt need in the international monetary system. Behind the very complex facade, what are the real needs to which the market caters? In the beginning, the main factor which encouraged the Euro-dollar market and stimulated its main location in London rather than New York was the so-called Regulation Q of the Federal Reserve System. Under this regulation, interest paid by US banks on time-deposits was fixed, while dollar deposits in foreign banks were not subject to an interest ceiling. In 1959, interest on off-shore deposits rose $\frac{1}{4}$ per cent above the Regulation Q level, and London banks came to bid for dollar deposits which in turn they re-lent to New York. The process necessarily starts with a balance in the books of a bank in the USA that is held by a foreign resident. This balance is typically a New York demand deposit held by a European bank, which has received it from a customer as the proceeds of a sale to the USA. The European bank òffers the dollar balance as a loan to a broker in the Euro-dollar market in London, who marries the offer to the requirement of (a) another non-US bank, (b) an international trading entity or (c) any acceptable undertaking requiring use of a dollar balance. Transactions are large. Borrowers and lenders are often banks or financial agencies. The period of the loan may be very short-term or as long as three months. The obligation of a borrower is to repay by a cheque drawn on a bank in the USA. Thus has grown up an elaborate process of financial intermediation, highly profitable to the links in the chain by reason of the interest differentials between borrowing and re-lending. By 1968, $30.4 billion in US currency was outstanding by European banks and $7.3 billion of five other currencies. By 1976, the comparable figures had risen to $224.0 billion and $81.3 billion respectively.

At the inception of Euro-currency dealing, London was the chief centre of the market. The concentration of merchant banks, non-British banks, discount houses, short-term money markets, provided not only a wealth of expertise but also banking institutions which quickly sprang forward to claim a share of the brokerage

Table 7.1   **External assets and liabilities of banks in some reporting countries, 1976 ($bn)**

	Domestic currency	*Foreign currency*
France		
Assets	1.5	48.0
Liabilities	3.8	48.7
Germany		
Assets	25.9	14.3
Liabilities	17.4	13.7
Italy		
Assets	0.3	12.3
Liabilities	1.4	15.0
Netherlands		
Assets	4.2	22.0
Liabilities	4.1	19.6
United Kingdom		
Assets	1.8	138.0
Liabilities	7.1	148.6
Canada		
Assets	0.5	17.1
Liabilities	2.0	14.6
Japan		
Assets	2.1	19.6
Liabilities	1.9	27.2
United States		
Assets	78.8	1.8
Liabilities	69.8	0.8

SOURCE: BIS, *Annual Report*, 1976–7, p. 106.

and intermediation profits. But the foreign banks in London, particularly the Canadians, were quick to earn profits there and to spread their expertise to other centres, and major Euro-currency markets now exist in Canada, Singapore, Japan and the Caribbean. The markets in Euro-currencies are highly developed and have become a large source of short-term credit. For many countries, foreign-exchange operations are now conducted, so far as the inter-bank market is concerned, through Euro-currency dealings. This is reflected in the fact that for many countries external assets and liabilities of banks are in currencies other than their own. Table 7.1 gives comparisons for a sample of countries. Not only has the volume of Euro-currency dealing burgeoned but institutional innovations have widened its scope. In the 1960s a retail side developed in the market, in that American banks in London (and also some London financial institutions) began issuing Euro-dollar certificates of deposit for amounts in excess of $25,000 for a period of one to six months. In the later 1960s the Euro-bond appeared. This is 'a bond underwritten by an international syndicate and sold in countries other than the country of the currency in which the issue is denominated'.[1] Euro-bond quotations and yields are collated and published by the Association of International Bond Dealers, which was established in 1969 and includes over 350 institutions. By 1975, $8 billion annually was being raised in Euro-bonds. Thus the Euro-currency market now covers the whole time-spectrum of borrowing and lending, from days to years. They provide an alternative and an extension to domestic money markets and impel countries to regard their interest-rate policies in an international setting. The market represents a venue of borrowing and lending outside the regulations and limitations of national monetary systems. It provides higher yields on mobile short-term international capital than the old asset forms such as US or UK bank deposits or Treasury bills. Many national central banks now hold part of their foreign-exchange reserves in dollar-deposit claims in this market. Aware of the advantages in yields and in the fostering of business contacts, large banks in main financial centres have fostered, augmented and refined the market until it has become a superb mechanism of international banking intermediation. Countries which once had only stable but parochial banking systems now have access to the capital resources of the world.

As an unsought-for incidental the market has played a considerable role in international balance-of-payments dynamics. It has enlarged the stock of international liquidity by providing dollars, partly from the convenient deficits of the United States and partly from borrowing from the US private financial sector. Thus the leading reserve and intervention currency has been made available other than through the more conventional balance-of-payments channels.

Perhaps the most interesting and spectacular achievement of the Euro-currency market was the recycling of funds from surplus to deficit countries during the payments problem which arose as a

[1]This definition is that of Morgan Guaranty, the investment bankers.

result of the first oil crisis in 1973–4. In 1973, after a general upturn in prices and activity in the previous year, there was a simultaneous sharp rise (48 per cent) in (non-oil) world commodity prices. Oil prices rose concurrently, and by December 1973 the price of crude was 150 per cent above that of October 1973. The rise in imported crude by mid-1974 in the USA was 233 per cent. Thus a general economic expansion, a primary-commodity inflation and an unprecedented rise in the price of oil combined to transform the balances of payments of the oil-importing industrial countries and the oil and primary commodity exporters. Although the non-oil primary-product inflation was short-lived, that of oil was not, and the whole of the 1970s was a difficult period in world payments. In 1974 the OPEC export surplus was $55 billion; in 1975 it was $32 billion. The deficits of the oil importers corresponded. Exchange rates could not do much to adjust such a deficit. The demand elasticities of the oil-importing countries for oil and of the OPEC countries for manufactured imports were very low in the short term. Relative prices could do little to adjust such a deficit. In any event there was no exchange rate through which relative prices of the surplus and deficit countries could be expressed. Oil was sold on world markets for US dollars and no exchange rate existed between the OPEC countries' currencies and the US dollar. The distribution of the total deficit among the oil importers was susceptible to the exchange rates between them, but we may ignore that fact for this discussion. There was in fact an enormous accumulation of earned dollars in the hands of exporters. How were the deficit countries to match this and adjust their deficits? The IMF's prescription was simple and, in the circumstances, constructive. It was that (a) countries should not try to adjust the deficits in their current accounts by deflation, but should (b) finance the deficits by external borrowing, preferably from OPEC countries. The IMF prescription was aimed at avoiding the general recession which would result from countries following the deflationary route[1] and at preventing a general redistribution of world international liquidity in favour of the OPEC countries. Since these countries were amassing a vast holding of US dollars from oil

---

[1] It should be remembered that some measure of recession was inevitable in any event as the demand required to purchase necessary oil and energy was switched away from other goods and services.

sales, it was natural that these countries should lend their earnings to the deficit countries. Finally this view was supported by the belief that the surplus of OPEC countries would not be permanent. Rises in their respective GNPs would induce imports. In the long run the demand of the oil importers for oil would decline as efficient substitutes were found. Also, OPEC countries might be induced to spend some part of their surplus in the form of aid to the poorest countries of the Third World. The OPEC surplus was seen as an international payments problem of perhaps a decade's duration, extendable by further rises in the oil price or some new twist of fortune in power politics. It was a plausible and, in the event, not inaccurate model.

The adjustment aspect of the model was particularly plausible. With OPEC countries amassing dollars in exchange for their oil, the dollars could only be spent on imports, or saved, the savings being invested in foreign money markets. So the OPEC surplus on current account was certain to be offset by its lending on capital account. Given that this condition was met, two other conditions were necessary: first, the surplus had to be lent among the deficit countries in a distribution appropriate to the size of their deficits; and, second, switches of assets between deficit countries had to be such as could be handled smoothly by financial institutions and markets. These two latter conditions came to be known as the 'recycling' problem and the 'switching' problem.

Optimal recycling required that each deficit country should have loans on capital account in dollars equal to the oil deficit it was running. Two main capital markets existed for the investment of surplus dollars, the British and American, and in these, in 1974, 35 per cent of OPEC surplus dollars were invested. For distributing dollars among the deficit countries in proportion to their deficits, either such countries had to earn dollars by surpluses with non-OPEC countries or they had to borrow dollars from the supply available at large in OECD capital markets. Both these things happened. Swings in balances of payments among oil-deficit countries did serve to redistribute dollars, and on these swings changes in exchange rates (under the now-floating market) may have played some role. But the main recycling took place through re-lending. In 1974 and 1975, $32 billion was lent by the oil countries as deposits in Euro-currencies. This formed a base for new lending of Euro-currencies to non-OPEC countries. It is certain that a large part of this went to oil-deficit countries either in the developed or the developing world. Finally there was some planned recycling through the IMF and the World Bank.

A striking aspect of the recycling process was the part played by the private institutions of the capital market. In this, the most serious disequilibrium suffered by the international monetary system for decades, there was major recourse to the private-sector capital markets and only secondary recourse to the IMF. This was made possible by the greatly increased scale and scope of the international capital market, in particular the Euro-currency market. It also reflected changing preferences of national monetary authorities. Whereas in times past a deficit not coverable by reserves was met by an appeal to the IMF for stand-by credit or currency exchange, this was now short-circuited by borrowing in the private market abroad. Although such loans had a high cost in interest they freed the monetary authority from the policy constraints which the IMF was likely to impose as a condition of providing such facilities. This left the IMF as a lender of last resort either for developing countries or, in the event of strain, on the private institutions. As we shall later see, strains did arise and the switch to private-sector financing had its dark side, but in principle and given strict banking practices it was constructive and it was a new and promising feature made possible by the new Euro-currency markets.[1]

Thus far we have drawn attention to attributes of the Euro-currency market which are, in the main, beneficial, stressing its intermediation, international liquidity and recycling functions. Two somewhat more arbitrary aspects of the market are important, since they are relevant to what we have already called the 'switching' problem. These are the size of the total Euro-deposit market, and how, if in any way, it can be controlled.

Switching is an inevitable movement between asset holdings of different types as the profitability and prospects of the assets change. In this context the switching is between various curren-

---

[1] The 'switching' problem raised by the oil deficit and referred to above did not in the event cause difficulties. It had been thought that large amounts of oil-surplus money deposited in London might be switched without warning to other financial centres, and that the size and uneasiness of international capital movements would become unmanageable. Such did not prove to be the case during the oil crisis, but the switching problem in a general sense is significant and will be referred to later.

cies, held either as investment venues, tax or safety havens from temporarily threatened alternatives, or as working or cash-flow balances. Progressively as the international monetary system has grown, and particularly in the post Second World War period, switches between currencies have become troublesome, threatening disfavoured currencies' exchange rates with devaluation, conferring unwanted strength on temporarily favoured currencies. Switches are frequently speculative, anticipating a profitable future change in a currency exchange rate. Under the adjustable-peg system of Bretton Woods days (1946–71) such speculation was frequent and destablishing to many currencies. Since switches in and out of currencies may be resisted by counter-selling or buying of a national currency by its own exchange fund, the size of the speculative 'fund' is crucial. It was once possible for a national exchange fund successfully to resist speculative attacks, assuming the fund to be adequately endowed with a balance of the intervention currency. Interpretations of adequacy might differ but the ability to resist prolonged speculative selling of the currency was certainly present for some currencies in the 1950s and 1960s. During the 1970s and strikingly in the 1980s it has often been impossible for single exchange funds to resist speculative attack for long. The international capital float from which purchase and sale of a currency can now take place is too large. Prolonged exchange depreciations and overshooting of the supposed purchasing-power parity under floating rates, has been the result of the huge supply of migrant funds against whose movements the reserve holdings of individual countries are inadequate. Two features render this inevitable: the ease with which in an international capital market funds may be shifted, and the amount of the funds available. For both of these factors the Euro-currency market is important. It provides a huge and seemingly ever-growing pool of funds offshore which can at any juncture move in or out of currencies to which such a move is temporarily profitable. The switch of funds to the United States in 1984–5, which has strengthened the US dollar to a level far greater than its equilibrium rate, is an example. The only way in which West European and Canadian governments could protect themselves from the depreciation of their currencies against the dollar would have been by a concerted selling of dollars simultaneously by all their exchange funds. The Bundesbank (central bank of West Germany) attempted alone to protect its currency, but failed. Only a group of major central banks acting together might have succeeded. It seems we must recognise currency switching as a general problem, exacerbated by the smooth working of the now-huge capital and exchange market, and controllable only by joint action.

We turn to two final aspects of the Euro-currency market which we may deal with together: size and control. Anxiety has often been felt that the supply of Euro-currencies grows continually but is not, like national currencies, under the control of a central currency authority. Size appears to worry some observers simply because size is associated in their minds with instability. The worry is size *per se*. A more sophisticated qualm is that since the holdings of Euro-currencies represent a part of international liquidity, their increase is in some way analogous to an increase in M1 or M2 for international money and will create proportionate world price rises. The reasoning behind this claim need not worry us a great deal. The net liquidity creation of Euro-currency deposits is small. Since such deposits are almost entirely of an inter-bank nature and since there is little transformation in the degree of liquidity of claims, new deposits are merely replacing old maturities. The liabilities of financial intermediaries in the market are about as liquid as the claims. If liquidity were really growing it would certainly be arguable that the consciousness of an increasing world stock (providing it was optimally distributed) would encourage countries to tolerate deficits and allow inflation to continue or increase. Since, however, the net addition to liquidity is small this fear may be discounted.

There is another reason why excess-liquidity creation in Euro-markets is not of such consequence as might at first appear. The majority of Euro-currency deposits are inter-bank claims: only those which are non-bank claims can qualify as liquidity. Of these, part are held by domestic residents and are included in the money stock of the reporting country. Only deposits held by non-residents which are non-bank deposits can be regarded as a net addition to national monetary assets.

Also germane to the question of size is that of control. It is now fairly widely agreed that Euro-currency deposits, if treated as money and if subject to the principles of fractional reserve banking, can be created according to some deposit-creating multiplier.

The question, then, of what governs the process of increasing Euro-currency reserves and the multiple deposit creation that arises from them, is an interesting one. This, of course, has to be considered for each currency for which there is an offshore market. Suppose the currency to be US dollars. The standard formula for induced deposits in a deposit-creating system is

$$\Delta D \quad = \quad \frac{1}{1 - e\,(1 - p)}$$

where ΔD in this case is the multiplier increment of created Euro-dollars, e is the proportion of dollar credits redeposited in Euro-banks, and p is the reserve ratio expressed as a fraction of Euro-deposit liabilities. For this equation ΔD is positively related to e and negatively related to p. In the Euro-dollar market, p, the reserve ratio, is low, while e, the redeposit rate, is also low, thus ensuring, with such values, a low rate of change of created Euro-dollars and hence a low deposit-creation multiplier. If we apply likely values as co-efficients in the equation (say 3 per cent as a reserve ratio and 15 per cent for the proportion of dollars redeposited – that is, a very high leakage from the Euro-currency system – the change in Euro-deposits from any injection is very low indeed at 1.16, signifying that any shift of dollars from the USA to Europe increases the total stock of deposits by little more than the amount of the transfer. Thus we may conclude that any single once-over transfer of dollars from the USA is little more than the size of the transfer itself. Only if there is a continuing transfer of dollars from the USA to Europe would the quantity of dollar deposits be increased without limit. Such a steady transfer is unlikely. Euro-dollar rates of interest are a pure function of supply and demand, and a steady expansion of the supply side would cause them to fall drastically. At the point where they equalled certificate-of-deposit rates in the USA, the flow would cease. Only at times when domestic deposit rates are uncompetitive is the transfer likely to be sustained. The lesson appears, then, to be that countries anxious for limited build-up of deposits of their currency offshore should add an additional dimension to their interest-rate policy to ensure that there is such a limitation.

(iv) International private-sector lending

We end this chapter on international capital movements with a brief discussion of a twin phenomenon – a great and unprecedented expansion of world international liquidity within the private banking sector, and expansion of the external debt of developing countries by amounts which seem uncontrollable. These debts have been accumulated for financing balance-of-payments deficits. They have been made possible by the development of the international capital market and have been a feature of the recycling process. The process is easily traceable after 1973 when non-oil developing countries began to finance their balance-of-payments deficits on commercial terms. Loans were given by banks, by banking consortia, and in the Euro-dollar market which was swollen with liquid dollar assets of the oil-exporting countries. Deficit countries delayed taking macro-economic measures to adjust their balances-of-payments deficits to the higher oil prices. They preferred to accumulate external debt in the private commercial-banking sector, which was more lenient in its conditions than the IMF, to which many countries were later driven when their debt burdens and deficits compounded and their foreign deficits persisted. A supply side within the banking system swollen by liquidity and competing for loans; a demand side composed of many countries in balance-of-payments difficulties, the consequences, large and profligate lending outside the limits of banking probity, inability by borrowers to repay and to service loans; a threat to international banking stability and a frenzied search for ameliorating measures.

All this goes back as far as 1973 and the first oil crisis, when many non-oil developing countries began borrowing heavily from commercial banks to meet balance-of-payments deficits. By 1982 a pattern had emerged. Aggregate debt was more than $600 billion. Table 7.2 gives a summary account of the growth of such debt. Thirty seven per cent of such debt was held by US banks, and three debtor countries – Argentina, Brazil and Mexico – accounted for more than 50 per cent of the total debt. Moreover, the exposure of US banks was great. Not only was the US share of the total debt large, but within the total figure 34 per cent was attributable to the nine largest banks in the United States. For example, Citibank's loans to Latin American countries amounted

Table 7.2 **Non-oil developing countries' external debt, selected years 1973–83 ($US bn)**

	1973	1976	1979	1981	1983
Total outstanding debt	130.1	228.0	396.9	555.0	664.3
Short-term debt	18.4	33.2	58.8	102.2	92.4
Long-term debt	111.8	194.9	338.1	452.8	571.6
To official creditors*	51.0	82.4	133.0	172.4	218.7
To private creditors	60.8	112.5	205.1	280.4	353.0
Ratio of external debt to exports of goods and services	115.4	125.5	119.2	124.9	144.4
Ratio of external debt to GDP	22.4	25.7	27.5	31.0	34.7

*Governments and international institutions.

SOURCE: *World Economic Outlook*, 1983. Compiled from various tables.

to 174.5 per cent of the bank's capital. Figures for a selection of other leading banks were: Bank of America 158.2; Chase Manhattan 154.0; Morgan Guaranty 140.7; Manufacturers Hanover 262.8; Chemical 169.7. All normal criteria of bank-lending security had been surpassed. For leading financial countries other than the USA a similar picture emerges.

During the later 1970s the accumulation of debt had caused little anxiety, but the onset of worldwide recession in 1979, another oil crisis and a worsening of recession brought matters quickly to a head. Recession reduced the exports of the debtor countries, the rise in oil prices worsened their terms of trade, their growth rates declined sharply.[1] In three of the largest debtor countries – Argentina, Brazil and Mexico – the decline was very sharp. When in August 1982 the Mexican Finance Minister announced that Mexico could not meet its debt-service payments, the impact of confidence was dramatic. Mexico was a large borrower but she was an oil exporter and she had been regarded as the most creditworthy of

[1]The growth rate of non-oil developing countries declined by 2.5 per cent in 1981 and 1.5 per cent in 1982; growth in the volume of exports fell from an annual average of 9 per cent in 1976–80 to less than 2 per cent in 1982.

Table 7.3   Developing countries: debt-service payments and amortization costs ($US bn: ratios per cent)

	1977	1979	1981	1982	1983	1984*	1985*
All developing countries Total debt-service payments	39.8	75.4	109.3	124.1	111.7	121.3	142.9
of which:							
Amortization	24.4	43.1	48.7	52.7	46.7	49.8	62.2
Interest	15.4	32.3	60.6	71.4	65.1	71.5	80.7
Debt-service ratio**	15.1	19.0	20.2	24.4	22.1	21.5	23.0
Non-oil developing countries Total debt-service payments	35.8	66.6	98.1	109.7	98.9	107.2	124.2
of which:							
Amortization	22.1	39.0	42.9	45.8	39.9	42.5	52.5
Interest	13.7	27.5	55.2	63.9	59.0	64.7	71.7
Debt-service ratio**	16.1	19.7	21.4	25.0	22.3	21.7	22.7

* Projections by Fund Staff.
** Payments (interest and amortization) as percentages of exports of goods and services.
SOURCE: IMF Survey, 7 January 1985.

the borrowers. The whole situation was now reappraised in a more depressing light. See Table 7.3. Loans to several countries needed re-scheduling; to others, loans would have to be made in order that debt-service could be met. The dreadful word 'default' was being used, albeit covertly, and a disaster model – that major debtors would combine in a 'cartel of default' – was being mentioned. 1982 and 1983 were dark years for many international bankers. Major defaults (*a fortiori* a cartel-imposed moratorium) would have threatened some of the greatest international banks, particularly in the USA. Last-resort facilities – the IMF, governments acting in consortia, etc. – were being canvassed.[1]

The crisis eased. The IMF dealt firmly (some would say cruelly) with the Mexican problem. Brazil was next on the list. Slowly and painfully these countries under IMF duress changed their domestic policies in order to give priority to adjusting their external deficits. The threat of collective action among the debtors passed. The contrast between the crisis atmosphere at the IMF annual meeting in Toronto in August 1982 and the euphoria at its counterpart in Washington in 1984 was striking. It seemed that once more the international monetary system had been able to roll with the punches and survive. The parameters of the debt crisis are clear. A huge supply of loanable funds was available from the earnings of the oil producers. A new and smooth mechanism was available for the distribution of these funds through the international capital market, and an insatiable demand for loans came from the developing countries, particularly the non-oil developing countries. The result was over-lending during a period when interest rates were extremely high and placed a growing burden on the borrowers. What reflections are prompted by this near-miss for disaster?

The first responsibility must be placed squarely on the international bankers who were at the heart of the recycling process. Some of the world's most illustrious banks lent vast sums to countries and for purposes which were never vetted for creditworthiness. The desire to lend and the fierce competition among banks to do so was a combination of profit motive and belief that there were rich pickings to be had in the field of foreign development lending. From the scanty writings that may be authentic,[2] the rumours and hearsay that surround individual cases, and the facts that emerge with time, a picture builds up that does bankers no credit when they are thus gripped by mass ambition.

A second reflection may be permitted on what was envisaged as the only solution should mass defaults on bank loans have taken

[1] A fairly clear picture of the dimensions of the debt problem may be had from William R. Cline, *International Debt and the Stability of the World Economy*, no. 4, September 1983, Institute for International Economics.

[2] A good and seemingly well-researched book on the lending boom of the 1970s is Anthony Sampson's *The Money Lenders. Bankers and a World in Turmoil* (Viking Press, New York, 1981).

place. A lender of last resort was to be sought – some financial colossus to whom a wounded Chase Manhattan, Hanover Trust or City Bank of New York might run for support and succour. No specific mentor was actually named but we may hazard a guess. The IMF came quickly to mind, but at once difficulties appeared. In 1982, when the loans crisis was at its height, the IMF was very short of funds and was endeavouring by an increase of quotas to increase them. It could not in its then condition have mounted a rescue on a sufficient scale. As a second possibility a consortium of central banks springs to mind. This might have been a starter, but since the main banks involved were American and West European there would have been some interesting negotiations in the run-up to such an operation. Moreover, would there have been time? Suspension of payments by a major bank or group of banks might have started a financial panic, affecting wider and wider banking circles before the steadying effect of even a multi-central bank consortium could have exerted a pacifying influence. No doubt the Bank of England, skilled in the politics of 'financial detachment' since the days of the Baring crisis – and, at the time we are discussing, fresh from its successful intervention to sort out the financial tangle resulting from the hostage crisis in Iran – would have been a prime mover in any support operation. The whole question of whether the international monetary system requires some central lender of last resort – whatever that should be, an augmented IMF or a central bank consortium – is clearly a matter to be pondered, especially if private-sector international lending continues at a high level.

(v) Conclusion

The place of the capital account in the balance of payments can now be reappraised. From being conventionally regarded as a subservient section of the total account with, at best, a long-term adjustment role, it must now be seen as the seat of prime-moving changes which, for the major countries, tend to make it a pacesetter for international monetary events. The features which justify this statement may be stated in general terms, with their historic examples in their context. We have written much of balance-of-payments theory on the assumption that it is concerned with the adjustment of the current account. We have now to recognise that the problem has come to be, to a great extent, what we may call the financial items of the balance rather than in the trade items.

First, capital movements engendered by international assessments of speculative gain, economic security, or political and non-economic forces, are not new. They have played a role in international finance at least since 1918. But in the modern setting they have grown enormously in volume, and because of instant information are quickened and facilitated. Funds move in a world setting, in a world capital market, according to switching criteria and planned portfolio distribution undreamed of fifty years ago. To accommodate these capital changes the current-account trade items must alter compensatingly, but since they cannot do so in the short term it is the exchange rate which must change – not always in a way convenient for trade or for domestic macro policies.

Second, speculative capital movements are now potentially so large that a single country whose currency is under speculative attack can no longer hope to hold sufficient reserves of intervention currencies to defend itself. The tide is now too powerful for one central bank to swim against it. It is this, more than any other force, which had caused currencies to 'overshoot' in value on the foreign-exchange market. The result has been periods of under-valuation or over-valuation of certain exchange rates as the world market probes uncertainly for the real parity value of the exchange rate. This experience has been demonstrated by sterling, the Deutschmark and US dollar on notable occasions in the 1970s and 1980s.

Third, there is the demand for a key currency, recognised as such and as the most desirable currency to hold, and to which the balance of payments of the key currency must conform. This is a special case of Robert Triffin's famous prescription that, subject to the maintenance of international confidence, the key-currency country must preserve a balance of payments in moderate deficit on current account – thus making its currency freely available. True, but this must now be extended and posed as a capital-account prescription. For a key currency universally desired either as a preferred currency for security reasons or for holding for profit, including that profit coming from higher interest rates, it is inevitable that the movement into the currency shall create either a rise in the exchange rate or a deficit in the current account, or some mix of both. This was the case of the dollar problem of 1984–5. In practice it has demonstrated how fiscal policy within a key-currency country, pursued independently of its key-currency position, can have deleterious effects on exchange rates for other countries and dictate to them macro policies which may run counter to their domestic needs.

Fourth, there is the prospect, indeed the necessity, that private-sector lending to developing countries should continue. It is a valuable source of development capital, an addition to second-line international liquidity. It should be a feature of the banking systems of mature countries. The danger that is posed by ill-considered lending by over-liquid and profit-hungry banks might be met by some self-policing within the banking systems themselves. Large loans by single banks or consortia loans by groups might be subject to scrutiny (but not veto) by some appointed group[1] within the banking fraternity capable of offering advice. This should not, however, be extended to any form of government control. The political implications of, say, the US government scrutinising or influencing loans projects by US banks to Latin America or Eastern Europe, are too obvious to need examination. The risk elements which deserve attention in future are (a) individual banks in particular countries accumulating loan risk exposure to a narrow group of borrowing countries, and (b) in a wider sense, the exposure of the whole Euro-currency market to risk from a concentration of loans to a few large countries. Loan concentration and country risk exposure should become the increasing concern of banking regulatory agencies in potential lending countries.

---

[1]One obvious method would be for central banks (say in the Basle Club) to work out a code of safe-lending which individual central banks could then enforce within their own banking systems.

8

Control of the International Monetary System

(i) Introduction

In Chapter 2 we said that control of the international monetary system was a prerequisite of its survival. We argued there that 'there must be some power at the centre of the system to influence its working', and we expressed the view that the record of the international monetary system over the past century demonstrated in its ups and downs the extent to which from period to period such power had existed and functioned. In this chapter we must examine these views more closely, conscious of the fact that we have now arrived at the most intractable decision – set in the whole international system.

Begin by simplifying to the point of naivety. There are two sets of problems involved: the political or purely control and administrative issues; and the technical economic and monetary issues. The first question, then, is, to whom are these matters to be allocated – politicians or economic specialists? The answer, of course, is that *de facto* the allocation goes willy-nilly to the politicians, the assumption being that only these Platonic 'philosopher kings' can make the decisions; that economic decisions are too important to be left to economists. Unfortunately the arcane mysteries of international monetary economics have not often been part of the training of the retired film stars, trade unionists, businessmen, lawyers and philosophers *manqué* who govern us nowadays. Nor are their executives well informed. The motivations of the politicians are, in this field , much as they are in others – power, influence, public acceptance and short-run political gain.

To some, and at some times, international finance is a legitimate medium for extension of power. More often, deliberate rational decision-making goes by default for lack of knowledge or opportunity. Nevertheless, it would be a monstrous conceit to argue that international economic decision-making should be delivered into the hands of the technocrats. There are frequently issues involved which are normative and transcend the merely technical. The division of decisive power between the political authorities and the technical advisors is a problem too abstruse to deal with here. Let us be content with a reflection. Economic decisions, particularly in international finance, are not well made in the hubbub of media-wide discussions. The glare of publicity illuminates their political rather than their scientific attributes. It is not without significance that recent history gives us examples of successful economic performances driven by obscure decision-making. The nineteenth-century gold standard was, at the time, neither understood nor widely noticed by politicians. Its decisions were made *sotto voce* by a few central bankers, most of whom were aware only of that small part of the whole system in which they operated. For a further example of success in an institution look at the European Payments Union (1950–59), which ordered the payments relations of the OEEC countries in receipt of American Marshall Aid in the years before general convertibility of West European currencies. This intricate set of arrangements was set up to widen regional convertibility of currencies. It achieved its aim, functioned efficiently, survived several minor crises, and was wound up as redundant when the currencies of its members became fully convertible. It functioned without notice or comment outside the field of payments, was directed and administered by sophisticates and was perhaps the most successful international financial institution ever created.

Although we cannot indulge in any lengthy discussion of the problems of political control of the international financial system, it is necessary to take the matter farther than its mention in Chapter 2. We bow to the fact that the political framework of decision-making in international monetary affairs transcends the purely technical. Before we turn to the latter we must have some reference map to which purely economic decisions may be related. In Section (ii) of this chapter we shall try to establish such a reference map. In Section (iii) we shall return to the purely economic issues of control.

(ii) Centralisation versus groups

At the heart of the political problem of controlling the international monetary system is the question of how to reconcile control from the centre with the national sovereignty of participant nations. The problem becomes one of compromise between centralisation and decentralisation. An extreme view of the international monetary system as analogous to a central banking system leads us to centralisation and an inevitable sacrifice of national sovereignty; a decentralised view of the system leads us towards a conception of the system as consisting of groups of nations within which what we may for the present call 'lesser' decisions can be made, leaving the inter-group decisions, which we may suppose to be of an overriding character, to be made as a result of inter-group negotiations. We have to examine these two views carefully: the choice between them is crucial.

The claim for the efficiency of a centrally controlled monetary system rests on several arguments. First is the frequently held view that any system which is centrally and strongly controlled is necessarily better than a system which is decentralised. Second, this is supported in the present case by the analogy of the national and the worldwide monetary system. Because the former is best controlled from the centre by a central bank it is deemed probable to certain that the international system will respond in the same way. Several leading economists have contributed to this view, by contrasting the slow development of the international system towards central control with the evolution of the British monetary and banking system in the nineteenth century.[1] The inference is that at some enlightened future time, when international federalism has been established, a world central bank of central banks will govern the system. Maybe so. In the meantime we live in a world of resurgent nationalism and no such condition is in prospect. There is also some doubt as to how far the analogy between national monetary system and world monetary system may be relied upon. In the former it is clear what is to be controlled: the money supply, the credit climate and the rate of interest. In the latter, is it the total of international liquidity, or exchange rates, or

[1]In 1967, commenting upon the Rio de Janeiro Agreement which established the IMF's power to create SDR's, Robert Triffin likened the international monetary system to the point in the nineteenth century when it was realised that the Bank of England could create money.

national macro policies, or capital movements, and in what mix and with what priorities? Moreover, in the domestic banking system the problems of control are far simpler. Unlike nation states in the world system, which resist any infringement of their national sovereignty, individual commercial banks in the domestic system submit willingly enough to the authority of the central bank. In the two fields in which that authority is applied, money quantity and interest rates, the authority of individual commercial banks is not necessarily thwarted. Their aims are profits, size, competitive power or whatever it is corporate firms strive for under competition. The central bank does not thwart these aims: it simply creates the climate in which they are pursued. Its directives condition the economic environment. In the world setting, where an international authority sought to control, say, the exchange-rate changes or the macro policies of individual states, there would be a clash of power, a curbing of authority in matters which individual states regard as their undisturbed province.

The more one considers the analogy between world control in some devised centralised system and national control in a central-ised banking system as we now know it, the more evident it is that the analogy breaks down. The matters to be controlled are diffe-rent qualitatively. It is the belief of this writer that, at this time in history, central control of the international monetary system is impossible. The historical evidence is all in that direction. The past twenty years have been a period of experimentation in economic policy, but all that has been at the national level. Monetarism and supply-side economics, creatures of the 1970s and 1980s, have been policies for purely national ends pursued against a narrowing focus of objectives. There has been a steady erosion even of the degree of internationalism which was implicit in Bretton Woods, GATT and the United Nations, a movement which even at its height fell far short of acceptance of the diminished national sovereignty implicit in a scheme for central control of the interna-tional monetary system. There has to be another way. There is no progress feasible on this route. The only alternative – that of decentralisation – must be explored.

There is a prerequisite for any alternative, namely that it arises naturally from the historical trend of events; that it is a develop-ment towards which it is possible to work and not some hypotheti-cal condition plausible only in a theoretical model. We are not concerned here with international utopias but with choices of routes along which the international financial system may be steered.[1]

The alternative to central control is to encourage the formation of national groups, a process which has been descernible for at least half a century but which has either been ignored or regarded as irrelevant to the large problems of the international financial system. The sterling area, which arose more or less spontaneously in 1931 and continued to increase in influence until the later 1950s, was regarded by the British at its centre as a tiresome responsibility and by the Americans as an undesirable vestige of imperial power. Bretton Woods, which conditioned much of our thinking on international financial politics between 1945 and the present, was theoretically based on the concept of equality of participant countries and their currencies, but in fact was dominated by the United States, with its key currency, the dollar, and guided after 1961 in major developments by the Group of Ten, its largest and most important members. The key-currency approach, canvassed by critics of the original Bretton Woods proposals as a series of currency groups ranged around key currencies, such as the pound, the US dollar, the French franc and others, would have led in a somewhat different direction. It is arguable that the underlying forces in the international financial system have led us away from the IMF's 'one country, one currency, all are equal, some are more equal than others' approach, in the direction of a group system the outlines of which are discernible. If so, it is possible to pick up and go on from here.

The outlines of the present grouping seem to be as follows. First there is the United States, whose currency, the dollar, is still the main world currency, fulfilling, albeit somewhat erratically, the functions of leading key currency. A number of countries, notably Canada[2] and some Caribbean states, hold their reserves and

---

[1]The trouble with economic utopias, whether in the single state or the international order, is that, while often excellent in themselves, we cannot answer the question, how do we get from here to there? There are no clean starts any more. We must work with existing institutions.

[2]The IMF (in *International Financial Statistics*) classes the Canadian dollar as 'independently' floating – a curious description since much of Canadian macro policy has, in the past decade, been concerned with maintaining a satisfactory parity with the US dollar.

regulate their exchange rate on the dollar. These, with the United States, we may regard as the 'dollar group'. Second, there is the European Monetary group, held together by the European Monetary Agreement and with formal agreed arrangements of their exchange rates in relation to the European Currency Unit (ECU). This group accounts for the major West European countries. Those, like Britain, which are not yet members may be well advised to join if the trend towards decentralised international monetary control develops. Third, there is a large group of countries, many in number but not in aggregate, accounting for a high percentage of world trade, which peg their currencies to external indicators – a group to the French franc, a group to the SDR, a group to some composite of currencies. These countries can be relied upon to follow whatever alignment suits them best. Realignments in great power groupings would redistribute the allegiances of such countries. It would be a long-term consideration as to whether such redistribution would be optimum for themselves or for the international system as a whole. Fourth, there is Japan, certainly not a group, but a single important trading country with a currency which has been strong since Japan's industrial recovery. Japan has been a surplus country. She has been under pressure on the currency front to reduce her surplus, and on the trade front to accept a higher volume of imports from other Western industrial countries. It will be a matter of concern in any decentralised system as to where she places herself. For the moment she is important enough to be regarded as an entity in herself.

It would be tempting to distinguish a fifth group of Third World countries but it would be unrealistic. The so-called Third World is too multifarious in interest, diverse in strength and economic objectives, to form a composite currency group. Many would distribute themselves according to the set of groups already given. For some, external trade is still of a magnitude to make currency or financial allegiances deferrable until good working arrangements become apparent. Yet another discernible group is that of the USSR and the Eastern bloc countries. These control their exchange rates and manage their foreign trade in accordance with their own economic plans. Their currencies are not vehicle currencies in the sense that they are in general use in world trade or their prices quoted in foreign-exchange markets. They have not, hitherto, played any active role, constructive or destructive, in the international financial system as we have discussed it in this book. Nevertheless, it may not always be so. Should they decide to move towards greater participation in the wider international monetary system, their interests and aims might have sufficient similarity to give them cohesion and bargaining status.

This grouping is tentative. It represents merely the sort of alignments towards which we appear to be tending, but, like any system, it oversimplifies and there are loose ends. Some important countries are hard to assign – Britain, Mexico, Brazil and others. But they themselves have the decision and must weigh options accordingly.

Given that some such groups establish themselves, what then? Within each group there would typically be either a common currency or some leading currency held as reserves and between which and the other currencies a stable exchange rate existed. Such arrangements would be tight and formal, approaching that of a single currency, or rest at least initially on working arrangements, as did, for example, the sterling area of the 1950s. We might distinguish three prototypes for the groups: The European Monetary Agreement with a single accounting unit, the ECU, to which all member currencies are related; a close association of countries assumed to be at a transitional stage in process to economic union. The macro policies of the member countries require to be co-ordinated, the aim being to match inflation rates. In the event of serious divergences in inflation rates, then exchange rates within the group can be altered. In addition, capital movements between countries within the group may require regulation, the trick being to direct capital flows towards the persistent deficit countries and away from the persistent surplus countries. A second and looser prototype is that of the currency union type, of which the EPU (1950–59) is a good example. Here there is a looser association of countries existing for payments purposes only – using a formal accounting system for intra-country clearing in terms of a defined and distinct unit, with periodic settlements in which earned units and units outstanding have to be honoured in terms of an agreed actual currency. Such unions are complex in detail but straightforward in principle. The success story of the EPU encourages the adoption of similar mechanisms in the future. The third prototype is that of the currency bloc, of which the old Sterling Area and French franc area are examples. Here the association is looser still, and is simply based on a key currency, held as reserve by such countries as, by trading and financial contacts, find it convenient. Exchange rates between member currencies and the key currency are kept stable, but may be altered by member countries from time to time where necessary. Countries may join or leave the group at will. The present dollar area partakes of these characteristics. Canada, for example, holds the bulk of her Canadian Exchange Fund reserves in US dollars, and allows her exchange rate with the US dollar to vary only as it suits her current macro policies and trading position.[1]

The common feature of all these group associations is that, for two sets of decisions, those of the exchange rate and those of macro management, the loss of sovereignty for a member of the group is not to a single global authority whose motives are to individual countries often obscure and suspect, but to a closer co-operative group in which the problems are likely to be shared and understood and in which political considerations are transcended by the economic. The suspicions that at present many countries have of the IMF, its American proclivities and association with American policies, makes it, or indeed any global authority, a hopeless candidate for central decision-making on either of the two variables mentioned. We do not say that these difficulties would be absent from regional or group decisions – indeed, the experience of the EMS indicates they would not – but we do believe that decision-making would be easier within the framework of a smaller group, especially if the decisions could be confined to a purely technical framework as they were in EPU.

The effect of a group system along the above lines would be to establish two distinct layers of decisions for the major variables, exchange rates and macro policies: within the groups and between the groups. First of all, however, we must remind ourselves of why these decisions are important.

In essence, changes in exchange rates and changes in macro policies are the two main vehicles of balance-of-payments adjustment. Start with an obvious fact: the equilibrium exchange rate for a country's currency is a reflection of its domestic price level.

---

[1]Even this association is too close for many Canadians who deplore the loss of Canadian initiative which it implies. In these nationalistic times even the mildest loss of economic sovereignty is resented.

Granted this, it follows that the pattern of exchange rates ruling in an international economy (group or world of groups) in equilibrium is a reflection of the various price levels of participant countries. If all prices in the international economy move in unison, up or down, then equilibrium exchange rates do not change. If price levels move diversely, then exchange rates must alter to reflect the changing price levels. If a major objective of the international economy is to minimise exchange-rate changes then there must be co-ordination of macro policies in order to make price levels move together. To the extent that price levels cannot be co-ordinated by similar macro policies, the resultant movements of exchange rates must be accepted. This in turn raises the awkward question of how the changes in exchange rates may be allowed to manifest themselves – by free rates, by periodic discrete changes of rates or by some hybrid method seeking to combine flexibility with stability. We may conclude that some compromise may be sought, to stabilise exchange rates as far as possible by co-ordinating macro policies for price and income control, and accepting whatever residual exchange-rate changes are inevitable either by shortfalls in co-ordination, by speculative capital movements or any other reason. Hitherto in the international economy we have made no effort to co-ordinate national macro policies, but have forced ourselves to deal with the corollary, highly volatile exchange rates. Control of both exchange rates and macro policies would be a step forward in stabilising the international economy.

Return now to the question of adapting this dual control to our decentralised system. Within a group of countries, co-ordination of national macro policies is certainly easier than it would be in the world as a whole. The group as such is likely to have a common interest in group stability. It may be content, as the sterling area was, to achieve internal exchange-rate stability. It may, like the European Community, be seeking to go the whole hog and establish a single currency, accepting the necessity of identical price and income movements which would stabilise exchange rates and ultimately make them redundant. To be sure, even in a group of countries, co-ordination of macro policies is not easy. The difficulties that the EEC had in establishing the European Monetary Agreement attest to that. But the fact that it was achievable and that the path towards a common European currency is discernible, demonstrates to this writer that, within a group, far more is achievable in purposive action than is possible in the more diverse and variously motivated world setting.

The precise features that we must look for within the group are three:

(1) some co-operative machinery whereby members may be made aware and encouraged in the macro policies appropriate to group members for the time being;
(2) some machinery through which exchange rates between members may be pegged and, when necessary, changed; and
(3) some form of group international liquidity which individual members may hold as reserves and which may be used to support their exchange rates *vis-à-vis* other members.

These conditions can be met in two main ways: through an informal association of countries agreeing to act according to certain principles, forming a currency area; or through a formal structure, similar to the EPU or more recently the European Monetary Agreement. There is no reason to advocate one avenue rather than the other: there are instances of both having worked well in the past. Moreover, by allowing both forms to flourish, a process of evolution is possible.[1] In any exercise in international monetary reform there is the difficulty of transition from old system to new. By encouraging a flexible process of change with a number of variants we ease the difficulties inherent in getting from 'here to there'.

One feature of the group system cannot be ignored. Within a group there is likely to be a senior partner, either the key-currency country or the country which merely dominates by size, and trade

---

[1]There are differences between the two forms in the matter of decision-making. In the formal clearing union, where member countries accumulate debts and credits in the union and settle month-end balances in some chosen currency, the form and details of the union are complex and have to be settled in advance by intra-country negotiation. Once the machinery is established, countries must accept its working. In the informal association, decisions tend to be made as events present themselves and the system evolves by precedent and experience. Which method is more practicable? The balance of advantage is hard to assess.

volume. To a considerable extent the cohesion of the group depends upon (a) the acceptance of the lead country as such and (b) the recognition by the lead country of its responsibilities. We have seen these requirements asserting themselves in some of the groups already in partial existence: the unwillingness of France to accept the natural leadership of West Germany in the EMA; the limitations on British economic policies in the 1950s by reason of her leadership of the sterling area; the reluctance of Canada for closer economic association with the United States. These problems are likely to diminish with time. Non-conforming countries will have the choice of accepting the conditions within the group or of splitting off and going it alone – the latter being an increasingly perilous option.

(iii) Economic relations of groups

Turn now to the purely economic relations between groups in the wider international economy. We face an international monetary system with a reduced number of entities but with the entities themselves larger, perhaps having more political power within the system but having to reconcile conditions in the wider world to conditions within the group. The entities of the world group, like their smaller counterparts, are likely to be disparate in size and bargaining power. At the world level, as at the level of the group, the strategic decisions are going to be (a) exchange rates, (b) macro policies and (c) international liquidity.

In the field of exchange rates we will assume that a behaviour pattern similar to that of the 1970s will exist, namely that rates will be free to fluctuate but under the influence of national exchange funds, which will hold them by intervention for longish periods, allowing them to alter in response to structural changes in balances of payments. This system is still the best compromise between the impossible option of firmly fixed exchange rates and the undesirable option of absolutely free rates. But the system revealed shortcomings during the 1970s which would probably appear even in a world economy of groups, namely: (i) speculative pressure on main currencies; (ii) overshooting in moving from parity rate to parity rate; and (iii) sometimes rates determined not by purchasing-power parity (that is, relative prices) at all, but by massive movements in the capital account. These features have been a prime source of instability in the international monetary system since 1970. Their removal is a *sine qua non* of a better system. We leave their consideration to the last section of this chapter.

How may exchange-rate decisions between the major world groups be made? We may start with whatever wisdom the past offers us. First, it is apparent that major exchange rates cannot be negotiated.[1] The confusion involved in settling a new rate for the US dollar in 1971, the Smithsonian Agreement in 1972, and the subsequent Volcker and Paris agreements in 1973, demonstrated this. Second, it is obvious that exchange rates cannot be imposed by an international organisation. The loss of sovereignty would be unacceptable. This leaves only one alternative: exchange rates may be allowed to float, subject to national exchange-fund intervention, but an accepted code of behaviour for such intervention must be established and adhered to. A supervisory role could be played by the IMF in this, infringements of the code incurring the sanction of that body by the refusal of its resources to the offending member. There is some precedent for this approach to the exchange-rate problem. In 1936, after a period of disturbed relations between the USA and the UK over the actions of their exchange funds, and in prospect of still further trouble with the breakup of the Gold Bloc and an increase in the number of countries operating exchange funds to control fluctuating exchange rates, the UK, USA and France concluded the Tripartite Monetary Agreement which laid down principles for the operation of the three leading exchange funds. This agreement was moderately successful during the three years 1936–9. The war ended its operation but its success was certainly in the minds of Keynes and White in the run-up to Bretton Woods in 1944. Such a set of rules-of-the-game applied in the context we have been discussing would be between the leading groups of countries, which would be few in number and whose actions could be subjected by the IMF to the glare of publicity. Moral suasion, plus such sanctions as the Fund could apply to mavericks, would perhaps be sufficient.

The exchange rate cannot bear the entire burden of adjustment

[1] For example, such an exchange rate as that between the US dollar and Western Europe.

for balances of payments. Adjustment is also a problem of macro management of monetary and stabilisation policies of countries in the open system. If balance-of-payments equilibrium is to be preserved there must be co-ordination of such policies. Disparate macro policies for inflation control, growth or fiscal objectives can only by chance provide optimal balance-of-payments conditions. Purposive co-ordination of national macro policies has thus far eluded us. Blocks of surplus and deficit countries have emerged. There have been disputes over which shall inflate, which shall deflate. Negotiation has been insufficient to assign where the burden of adjustment lies. During the 1950s and part of the 1960s we enjoyed conditions peculiarly conducive to balance-of-payments stability even with fixed exchange rates, in that the general growth of the large industrial countries was at similar rates. Disparity in the rates was compensated for by periodic rate adjustments. But when in the later 1960s and in the 1970s rates of growth and inflation became diverse and when large capital movements asserted themselves, the exchange-rate system was under strain. The breakdown of Bretton Woods and the onset of floating exchange rates in the 1970s were the result. Even when exchange rates were freed, disparity of macro policies continued to destabilise the system. In particular, the position of the USA and its currency in the recession of 1975, the recovery and subsequent slide into deeper recession in 1979, and the recovery and resumption of growth in 1982–3, provided, because of the dollar's importance as key currency, a special case, which has to be dealt with directly we consider how to co-ordinate macro policies. Experience indicates that it is not good enough merely to get the directions right – to expand together or contract together. We have to get the rates of expansion right, and we even have to decide in the light of international considerations what policy tools are to be used – interest rates, credit policy, fiscal policy, exchange rates.

The behaviour of the United States, which in 1984–5 by an old-fashioned Keynesian injection pulled itself out of the recession more swiftly than any other country, and by an import of capital and an overvalued exchange rate escaped the consequences of its fiscal excesses – even to lowering interest rates in the face of the largest budget deficit ever recorded – all demonstrate what effects maverick behaviour by the leading key-currency country can produce in the international economy. To co-ordinate macro policies as to direction, pace, and policy tools is probably a pleasing dream. All that can be done is to set up machinery at the summit, that is between leading groups of nations, for consultation, and beneath the summit to have consultation and advice from technical agencies. This we have already, from the annual economic summits and from the IMF, OECD, the Basle Club and UN agencies. The knowledge of what is needed is usually forthcoming: the will to use it and act upon the advice is not. Economic summits have too often been political charades, with kudos going to the best actors.

Strategic decisions about international liquidity may be easier to make. We have some encouragement from the record. The IMF and Bretton Woods were originally set up in 1944 to supplement existing international liquidity. As prices and international trade volume have risen, measures have been continually taken to raise international liquidity. Quotas of the IMF have been increased eight times; the General Arrangements to Borrow were set up in 1961; SDRs were created by the Rio de Janeiro Agreement of 1967; several additional facilities were created by the IMF during the hectic days of crisis in the 1970s. There is every reason to suppose that international decision-making for international liquidity will continue in the future. Choice for development, in this writer's view, should be the SDR. The creation of that international unit was a significant step forward. Sixteen years later some progress has been made. The SDR is an international unit of account. Dealings in SDRs take place between central banks and the Fund. The problem is how to increase the qualified acceptability which it has achieved as an international money form. The technical problems of expanding the issues of SDRs, of making the unit available as a money-market asset, of how to give it the major not the minor role in national reserves, should all be examined by the IMF in an impartial review – that is, apart from the political views of some of its leading members.

There is one further topic which must concern us in this short review of control problems: the role of the IMF. The Fund is one of the principal legacies to us of the Bretton Woods system which expired as a result of the Nixon measures in August 1971. The fact that it is still on centre stage in the international system after forty years must surely indicate some utility in its existence.

The Fund has certainly had a checkered career. Born, in hope, to be the centre of the Bretton Woods system it was soon set aside as that system was held in abeyance until 1959 by the difficulties of the post-war period. It was lucky to survive that period when a whole set of international agencies – OEEC, in particular – took over management of a set of special problems. Saved by convertibility of currencies and the belated achievement of the Bretton Woods world, it was brought by an able Executive Director[1] into the centre of affairs. During an eventful decade in the 1960s it established itself, achieved some influence and, by the benefits it had to confer, it gained in power. When Bretton Woods ended in 1971 it adapted its policies to what it had consistently opposed, floating exchange rates. It continued to extend balance-of-payments aid to members, preached conservative rectitude in politics, lived in moderate peace with the USA and in troubled association with the ever-more-vocal Third World. In the 1980s it has had to live with Reagan, monetarism and supply-side economics, and through forcing its orthodoxy on debtor countries has become, to say the least, unpopular. Its greatest achievement is that it has survived. Even to scan its history is to see that this organisation has a stock of experience which alone is an argument for its retention.

Supplementation of international liquidity, influence over exchange rates, commentator on macro policies, policing of multilateral payments – these are the Fund's functions. It performs them all with some measure of success. In some, the shortfall from what is necessary is considerable. Take the functions one by one. In the field of international liquidity the present contribution is small – fluctuating in the past three years (1984–6) around 10 per cent. But it is capable through the SDR scheme and by increase of quotas, if members would sanction them, of a much larger contribution. The fact that major deficit countries resort to the Fund, despite swingeing policy conditions, demonstrates that it is playing an important role. It is a role 'at the margin' but, as has been said in economic theory, 'it is at the margin that the interesting things happen'.

In its influence over exchange rates the Fund is ineffectual. Changes are made without its approval. Major changes, even in the Bretton Woods days when its theoretical powers were stronger, have been made without its prior consent.[2] Now in the floating-

[1]Per Jacobsson.
[2]The French franc devaluation of 1948, the British devaluations of 1949 and 1967, the Canadian float in 1951, were all taken unilaterally by the governments concerned.

exchange rate era its surveillance of members' exchange rates
dates from April 1977, when principles for the guidance of members' exchange policies were adopted by the Fund. These principles are general and confine themselves to:

(a) condemning exchange rate manipulation which is deleterious
    to the economies of other members, particularly if it implies
    any element of competitive depreciation;
(b) advocating intervention by a country in the foreign-exchange
    market to prevent disturbing short-term fluctuations in the
    exchange value of its currency;
(c) charging members in their exchange intervention to take
    account of their operations, so far as they affect other mem-
    bers' currencies.

These principles, like condemnation of sin, are irreproachable.
The trouble is that in practice they are hard to apply, and that, in
the last resort, the Fund has neither the power nor the sanctions to
enforce them. So far as application is concerned, a country's
exchange-rate policies are only part of its wider macro policies for
the adjustment of its balance of payments and the control, through
demand management and monetary policies, of inflation. The
place and the priority of exchange policy in the wider policy mix is
therefore overriding and cannot be side-stepped by the Fund. In
some cases a country may wish its exchange rate to play the major
role of adjusting its balance of payments, in others it may wish to
follow macro policies for domestic price level or employment
purposes, which require an exchange rate to be held neutral or
even to play a role subsidiary to other policy weapons in pursuing
such policies.

It is possible to take one of two views of Fund exchange-rate
surveillance. Either it should be aimed (as it at present tends to be)
at a general oversight of all macro policies of member governments, their influence on the balance of payments, and their use of
the exchange rate to pursue domestic objectives, or it should be
narrowly focused – as is the implication of the 1977 declaration –
on the technical operations of the monetary authorities in the
exchange market.

As in all questions of IMF control over members' policies, it is
one thing to make rules, but quite another to enforce them. There

are only two sanctions which can be applied by the Fund against its members in the case of policies which it deems inappropriate. The first is that vague and ineffectual package of published criticism that is described as 'moral suasion', which sees members' policies as inappropriate, condemns them as such and draws public attention to their shortcomings. The best we can say of this sanction is that it is weak. The second sanction is in the control of policies by the Fund when it gives assistance to a member beyond the automatic first tranche of its quota. This sanction can be very real, as was demonstrated when the Fund gave assistance to the British in the mid-1970s. It is a considerable thing for weak Third World countries that are suppliants for aid. The trouble is that it is also a considerable deterrent to deficit countries which have a choice between the Fund and other sources of aid. The raising of international credit in the private-sector financial market has diverted from the Fund so much of its assistance and advice-giving role as to diminish its status at the centre of the international financial system.

(iv) Conclusion

In ending this chapter it is hard to avoid the conclusion that 'control' is the most potentially destabilising feature of the international monetary system. No system can be any better than the human beings who manipulate it. As in the general political sphere, ignorant or ill-intentioned leadership in the monetary system can wreck the system, especially if such leadership occurs in the key-currency country.

Try as we may, the answer to the question of how we may establish a system in which national sovereignties are overriden by central power, eludes us. Self-interest is obvious; the intricacies of international finance are subtle, attenuated, boring and mysterious to electorates. Exercises in international monetary reform are to governments as much occasions for defensive policies as are armaments negotiations or tariff bargaining. It is essential to approach such exercises in a realistic frame of mind.

It is a main thesis of this book that the international monetary system is always in crisis – crisis being defined as change. It is the necessity of monetary reform that change is controlled and advantage taken of such elements as are beneficial. In the field of control of the monetary system the following matters demand attention.

(1) It appears advantageous to recognise and take advantage of the proclivity of the international economy to split into groups. The decision-making of each group will then be conditioned by whatever forces brought the group into existence. Decision-making between the groups, while still difficult enough to negotiate, will at least be between fewer entities.

(2) The necessity for a power at the centre of the international system remains the most difficult requirement. The IMF has not and is unlikely to acquire the necessary power, still less the ability to enforce it. The best approach is to so perfect the general conception of the way the international system works as to inculcate in member governments a sense of the 'rules of the game' such as existed in the nineteenth-century gold standard. Constant refinement and stating of these rules and directing of publicity towards those who break them should be the task of the IMF.

(3) Does the IMF with its wide range of functions meet the necessity to have a force at the centre of the system? The answer is that it does not do so completely, but that it goes far enough towards it to warrant its preservation and development. The Fund's power and influence should be greater. Wider acceptance of the Fund could be fostered by eradicating the view that the Fund is an American creature and a vehicle of American policies; and by aligning its policies as much towards the Third World as towards the industrial north. The Fund must always have benefits to give to members so that withdrawal of such benefits acts as a sanction. Increasing recourse to the Fund by members, an extension of Fund lending facilities, an even-handed dispensing of assistance and advice, are the basis of more effective Fund operations.

9

Conclusion

(i) Strengths and weaknesses

The central theme of this book, if it has escaped the reader so far, is of an international monetary system which, while constantly adapting itself to change, has constant attributes which must be held in equilibrium if the system as a whole is to survive. The relations of these attributes may change, and this gives the system flexibility. But the attributes must all be present and work together if breakdown is to be avoided. So far, the teaching of history appears to be that the flexibility of the system is considerable. Thus even in the 1930s when the system came nearest to breakdown, for lack of direction and for weakness in the adjustment mechanism, the system bent but did not fracture. In the nineteenth century, when the elements were all present, the system worked as well as it has ever done, demonstrating its adaptability, albeit in economic conditions more tranquil than those which were to follow as the twentieth century unfolded.

We have examined the basic attributes of the system – international money, adjustment, institutions, the control problem – in their turn, trying to see what they are and how they meld into the system as a whole. We have glanced briefly at the historical record and discerned two features from which a threat to the stability of the whole system could come: either from a failure of one of the elements in the system – as with the lack of control of the system in the 1930s; or from a failure to realise the significance of institutional changes within the system – as with the great increase in the size and scope of the capital market and the weaknesses of the international banking system in the 1970s.

In this final chapter it is necessary to cast the whole problem of stability, as we have discerned it, in the context of the 1980s. What are the strengths and weaknesses of the system in the age of Reagan, Thatcher and Gorbachev?

The question is set purposely in these personal terms, for the ambience is all-important. The present is not a congenial environment for economic analysis or reform of the international monetary system. The world of Reagan and Thatcher seems not forty but light years away from Keynes, White and the rest, refashioning the system in the sensuous warmth of July 1944 in New Hampshire. What is in contrast is not scale, institutional change, or even knowledge of how the system works, but the contrast of intellectual backround and expectation. Then, there was a plan conceived against the backround of a theoretical conception. Divergences of opinion were as to implementation, timing and method. Now all that is lacking. In a bleak, intellectual desert, worthy of New Hampshire in January, it is deemed intellectually effete to argue that better economic relationships may be moulded and fashioned: better far to leave these matters in the hands of forces endemic to the system itself, working to produce conditions suitable for the regeneration of capitalism. Maybe so. But let us, all the same, take stock of the situation.

(ii) International money

First, what about the international money stock? For the present, the international liquidity problem, as we knew it in the 1950s and 1960s, is quiescent. The essence of that problem was that we came to rely for our international money dominantly on a single currency. Thus, for its quantity and its acceptability we found ourselves in the hands of a single country whose economic policies determined the efficiency of the key currency as such. The reversion to flexible exchange rates in the long run, eased the demand for international money, and the extension of private-sector credit as a form of second-line international liquidity has also been useful – though at some considerable cost in terms of stability. It is conceivable that the world may continue for a very long time to operate with a key currency, even with the US dollar, as international money. As long as certain policy obligations are met by the key-currency country, that is a sufficient condition for an effective supply of international money.

But we have already advocated that a growing volume of international fiat money is desirable – that the SDR system should be extended until that money form accounts for a large proportion, if not all, of the total supply. Perhaps this is mere fastidious tidiness, a desire to have the total international-money supply under one control. To extend the scope of SDRs it will be necessary to widen their acceptability, probably by establishing them as valid money media in national and international private-capital markets. Once this is done, switching between them and the other established wealth-holding media will be universally possible. Thus we will still be in a position where several money forms, currencies and SDRs among them, will be held for reserve and market intervention purposes. There will be nothing new about that. In the nineteenth century reserves were held in gold or sterling; in the twenty-first they may be held in SDRs or dollars or Euro-currency units. Switching may still be a problem, but it will be a problem which can be contained by manipulation of the SDR, its status and earning-power as a money medium. Above all it will mean that SDRs may be increased *pari passu* with the volume of world trade and the demand generated for them by balance-of-payments variation.

The prescription which appears to arise from scrutiny of the international-money element in the international monetary system is, then, the simple one of expanding what we may describe as the synthetic element in the total money supply – for practical purposes the SDR. At present this development is baulked by the majority required in the IMF vote for such creations, which places virtual veto power in the hands of the United States. Means must be found to link the creation of SDRs at least to the growth of trade. There must also be provision for *ad hoc* creations, in addition, to meet special contingencies. There is a strong political element in the decision-making to expand international liquidity. One recalls even as far back as the post-war years the US resistance towards proposals by many economists to increase the amount of international liquidity by increasing the US buying price for gold – a resistance based partly on a claim that to increase national reserves by this means would make countries more tolerant of external deficits and of inflation, but more probably on the benefit which would have accrued to the Soviet Union and South Africa as major gold producers. The argument that increased reserves raises the tolerance level of countries to inflation, has been used by Reagan to justify hostility to the further creation of SDRs. We must divest the decision-making process of these political overtones. Automatic reaction to specific indicators should condition the quantity of international money.

(iii) Adjustment

The thread that has run through all our discussion is that in the international monetary system we must have a mechanism of adjustment. Failure to provide one robs the system of stability. True, but then there remains the question, How may we judge the process of adjustment – deeming it efficient or otherwise? The traditional test of an adjustment mechanism was to apply to the balance of payments the criteria of an equilibrium system. The balance of payments was deemed to be in equilibrium if over a period sufficient to accomodate seasonal and cyclical variations there was no change in the international reserves of the country concerned. Shocks to this equilibrium, either exogenous or endogenous, had to be offset, or adjusted, either by some mechanism built into the system or by *ad hoc* policy measures of the government concerned. The nature of the long-term equilibrium was never in fact clearly defined. No long-term equilibrium theory of the balance of payments ever existed, but it was often inferred that the capital account of the balance of payments could play its part in such an equilibrium. Canada's balance-of-payments situation prior to 1914, for example, in which a deficit on current account was successfully offset by impact of long-term development capital, was regarded as stable and indeed exemplified a typical stage in the development of a country's external financial relations.

The role assigned to capital movements in traditional adjustment theory has, however, been a secondary one. The prime mover in balance-of-payments change was variation in the flows implicit in the trade account. Restoration of equilibrium implied forces acting on these flows – price changes, exchange-rate changes, income changes – to bring them to an appropriate new relationship. Capital flows might play their part (as they did in gold-standard procedural theory), but they were subsidiary to the changes generated in the trade account.

Since the Second World War and increasingly with the passage of time, disequilibrium has been initiated by changes in the capital account. If we consider the major structural problems in the international financial system over this period – the dollar problem between 1960 and 1973, the German surplus problem, the weakness of sterling in the 1950s and 1960s, the dollar problem of the 1980s – only the German surplus problem was a problem of the current account. The dollar has been subject to massive capital-account movements, first when American export of capital and government outlays abroad far exceeded the country's ability to generate an offsetting trading surplus, and latterly when high interest rates attracted capital from the world at large to finance the huge American budget deficit. The British sterling problem in the Bretton Woods period was that of recurrent speculative capital movements against the currency, induced by expectations of exchange devaluation. We may conclude that, at the least, capital-account changes are as important as changes in trade flows, particularly in view of the great expansion of the world capital market, the Euro-currency market and the ease and speed with which capital flows may now take place.

So the view of the adjustment mechanism changes. From Bretton Woods until the 1980s the view was that an adjustment mechanism was essential for correction of balance-of-payments deficits. In the absence of such a mechanism, and particularly if international liquidity were in short supply or maldistributed, then countries would resort to direct controls and protectionism, to the detriment of the multilateral nature of the international economy. In the context of the 1980s it seems more appropriate to view the adjustment problem as one of dealing with autonomous capital flows rather than trading-account deficits. The effects of unwanted capital flows may also be detrimental. Examples might be:

(1) An outflow of capital will have effects on the exchange rate and exchange reserves with implications for relative prices of traded goods.
(2) An inflow of capital may be encouraged by a country to fund a budget deficit or fiscal policy otherwise non-feasible.
(3) A fundamental disequilibrium in the current account may be masked by transitory capital movements thus confusing the real solution to a balance-of-payments problem.
(4) Speculative capital movements may make it impossible for a central bank to maintain an orderly foreign-exchange market.

(5) Capital movements made for mistaken or improvident reasons may build into the world system such instability and perversion as is impossible to correct.

It seems that a much broader conception of the adjustment problem is now forced upon us. We can hardly look to an automatically invoked adjustment mechanism, such as induced price or income changes, to adjust the balance of payments. Capital movements arise from many causes, and a much more variegated collection of policy measures is required to deal with them. Moreover, trade-balance deficits will continue and will require that price, income or exchange-rate changes will play their part when required.

Can we usefully generalise the measures with which disequilibrating capital movements can be met? If we divide such movements into short-term funds flows, either speculative or in search of higher yields, we turn naturally to interest rates as the manipulative device. The recipient country can discourage such inflows by reducing interest rates relative to other countries and net of the exchange risk involved, the countries losing funds will raise rates to try to retain them. This is and has long been a familiar process. But for capital flows such as those which have affected the US economy in the post-war period – the outflow of direct investment in the 1960s and the inflow of capital in 1984-5 – there can be no general solution. Such phenomena must be dealt with on their own terms.

Since adjustment processes must consist in large part of changes in monetary and/or fiscal policy by the countries concerned, there must be some means of ensuring that such policies are mutually constructive. Much historical evidence points to the fact that adjustment of an international disequilibrium may be frustrated either by disparate and unco-ordinated actions by the countries concerned or even by deliberate offsetting action by one country against another. Nowhere is the necessity for some form of international control more obvious than here, but nowhere is it more obviously difficult to implement. The whole issue of implementing such a control was discussed in Chapter 8, not with very satisfactory conclusions. We must, it seems, leave this question as the one which above all defies any realistic solution and threatens the stability of the international system more than any other. It may, as we have suggested, be by-passed rather than solved by encouraging the formation of commonly motivated groups of countries. Such a strategy would at least reduce the number (although not the potential danger) of policy clashes.

(iv) Exchange rates

The exchange rate system plays a major role in adjustment, but since the ordering of the exchange-rate pattern is such an important feature in itself we must summarize our ideas on it separately. We saw the choice of exchange-rate systems as now being a twofold one: between some variant of what we may call flexible rates and fixed rates of the adjustable-peg type. Any choice must involve some risks and disabilities and be the result of weighing a balance of advantage. The choice which we assess as optimal is one in which the exchange market is free but in which rates, in particular key rates between the major currencies, are held stable by central-bank intervention for periods of time. The aim is, then, to smooth the market and dispel short-term fluctuations but to allow structural changes to manifest themselves and have their effect on trade and industrial structure. Entirely fixed rates of the Bretton Woods type, and their opposite, entirely free rates, we regard as non-feasible systems; the former because structural changes in trade and balances of payments are frequent and cannot be reflected in a fixed rate, and because of the speculative pressures to which a fixed rate must necessarily be subject; the latter because of the uncertainties and trade disincentives which must attach to a wildly and frequently fluctuating rate. The problem is, therefore – within the spectrum of flexible rates – to discipline movements of the leading currencies so that at any time the exchange parities give a felicitous pattern of relative prices of traded goods.

The two elements of this discipline are (i) the intervention of national exchange funds in the market for smoothing purposes, and (ii) the initiation of 'target zones' of stable exchange rates. The intervention element has, of course, been with us since the early 1930s and, by now, leading central banks are well versed in the procedures. What is new, however, is that individual central banks cannot now exert the market leverage that they once did.

The scale of the exchange market and, in particular, the effect of large capital movements when they occur, are now so great that rate changes occur willy-nilly despite the leverage of a central bank, which lacks the size of reserves that is necessary for intervention. It is now essential that market intervention requires the power of a consortium of central banks, which begs the question of the unanimity of purpose which must exist in order to achieve this.

'Target-zones' of exchange-rate stability were an IMF conception put forward in 1974, when the Fund reluctantly recognised that flexible rates were a fact of life that had come to stay, and put forward some principles to govern their working. Key rates between major currencies, say the US dollar, the pound, French franc and Deutschmark, would be stabilised. Other lesser currencies could then stabilise relative to a major currency of their choice. The target-zone scheme which we would advocate differs from this somewhat, recognising the difficulty of stabilising at one fell swoop the most intractable currencies in the world (this seems so impracticable as to solve the problem by assuming it away) we would distinguish related groups of countries within which it would be possible to maintain stable rates of exchange. Rates between the groups would then have to be manipulated in accordance with some negotiated principles. In this way the greatest difficulty of managing exchange rates would be reduced to a few significant elements, namely the exchange rates between the groups.

Once more we return to the requirement of common macro policies as the prerequisite of exchange stability. Dictation of suitable macro policies by an international body is, we believe, impossible. The group system reduces but does not solve the control problem. It seems, however, to be the only alternative to leaving exchange rates to find their own level and accomodating ourselves to the result as best we can. In this case they become a powerful variable to induce instability with every change exogenous or endogenous.

(v) Final conclusion

The final conclusion is the most general one we can draw from the discussion: there is evidence to lead us to believe that the international monetary system is far more stable than seems so at first sight. At a popular level, the news media, when short of other material, delights in threatening a 'breakdown of the international monetary system'. By this they would appear to mean a collapse of major monetary institutions, a failure of the price system, and a return to barter either through fast inflation or a universal unacceptability of currency and saving media. From this disaster model we are abjured to turn away in fear and trembling.

The writer finds it hard to share such fear. The international system began unconsciously, and grew as the world economy grew. Once we became conscious of it as such we assumed responsibility for it, and economists have accumulated a vast amount of data and some impressive theory to analyse its functioning. In the light of this knowledge we have passed to the view that we can control the system and mould it to our needs. The problems of doing this are political rather than economic, for the decision-making which is involved in reforming the system, in simplifying it or in making it more efficient, cuts across the interests of participant countries as politicians interpret them. In fact, the international monetary system has experienced what we have called international monetary crises, but these are rather changes of direction than threats of imminent breakdown. The switch from gold-backed currencies to fiat currencies related by market exchange rates took twenty years to achieve, that double-decade spanning the greatest war and period of social and political confusion that the world has experienced, but there is a continuity from the world of 1924 and the return to gold and the Bretton Woods Agreement of 1944 that certainly does not look like collapse or breakdown. The same elements are there playing their parts in similar ways: the same problems present themselves, the jargon of discussion changes but not the agenda. The economic variables and their manipulation is not a different problem. Ricardo, Marshall, Viner, Keynes and Meade could sit at the same table today and have a mutually meaningful discussion.

On the political side the future is menacing. The international monetary system has become more political at the same time as huge increases in scale have taken place. While the decisions to be taken have not altered, the scale of the coefficients for the variables involved has grown. The implications of mistakes, misjudgements, or decisions taken for political advantage, are far greater than in past years. Moreover, modal points have developed within the system. What happens at the US Treasury and Federal Reserve has great significance for the world at large. The policies of EEC carry implications far outside Europe. How can we ensure that policy-making at these modal points can be of quality to match the scale? We cannot. The instability that exists in the international monetary system is the instability inherent in scientific knowledge, on the one hand, and how to apply it, on the other. It is exemplified in its direct and most pressing form in the relation between physics and physicists, on one side, and world leaders, unstable, ambitious, purblind, on the other. There is no reason to suppose that politicians will do what economists tell them, any more than we can hope that the White House or the Kremlin will listen to the professors.

Index